TAKE CHARGE
of
YOUR EMOTIONS

TAKE CHARGE
of YOUR
EMOTIONS

SEVEN STEPS *to*
OVERCOMING DEPRESSION,
ANXIETY, *and* ANGER

DR. LINDA J. SOLIE

BETHANYHOUSE

a division of Baker Publishing Group
Minneapolis, Minnesota

© 2013 by Linda J. Solie

Published by Bethany House Publishers
11400 Hampshire Avenue South
Bloomington, Minnesota 55438
www.bethanyhouse.com

Bethany House Publishers is a division of
Baker Publishing Group, Grand Rapids, Michigan

Printed in the United States of America

Library of Congress Cataloging-in-Publication Data
Solie, Linda J.
    Take charge of your emotions : seven steps to overcoming depression, anxiety, and anger / Dr. Linda J. Solie.
        pages cm
    Includes bibliographical references and index.
    Summary: "Respected Christian psychologist provides practical ways for readers to improve their emotional health, focusing on depression, anxiety, and anger"—Provided by publisher.
    ISBN 978-0-7642-1113-3 (pbk. : alk. paper)
    1. Emotions—Religious aspects—Christianity. 2. Depression, Mental—Religious aspects—Christianity. 3. Anxiety—Religious aspects—Christianity. I. Title.
BV4597.3.S65 2013
152.4—dc23   2013016378

14 15 16 17 18 19 20   8 7 6 5 4 3 2

To my parents, Bill and Judy Solie,
with gratitude and love

Contents

Contents

Acknowledgments

I want to thank a number of people for contributing to this book, beginning with my parents. They provided me incredible support throughout this entire journey. My mother, Judy, fixed me countless meals so that I could devote Fridays and Saturdays to writing with minimal interruption. She also carefully reviewed the manuscript, as did several people who generously shared their professional expertise, including my father, Bill, and my brother, John Solie, retired and current pastors, respectively; psychology professor Pat Frazier, author Nancy Nordenson, and entrepreneur Jim Carlson.

I am very grateful as well to Bethany House Publishers, and especially to acquisitions editor Tim Peterson for taking a risk on a first-time author and, with wisdom and kindness, guiding me through the publishing process. He, Christopher Soderstrom, and Nancy Renich have thoughtfully and skillfully refined this work at each editorial stage. I've been privileged and blessed to work with this talented team.

And I want to express thanks to others who contributed in a variety of ways to this final product, including Marilyn Anderson, Marti Anderson, Jim and Kris Bruckner, Erin Carlyle,

Griffin Clausen, Lynette Clausen, Brian and Nancy Cripe, Luke and Elvira Englund, Nancy Gustafson, Betty Hall, Don Holt, Jeff and Barb Johnson, Sherrill Nelson, Mark and Carol Rholl, Chris and Catherine Solie, Holly Solie, Lee and Asta Solie, Matt Solie, and Stephanie Wendt. Most of all, I thank God, who created our emotions, for his guidance on how to manage them, and for orchestrating this entire adventure.

Introduction

Many people believe their genetics or brain chemistry doom them to a life of emotional pain. Moods descend on them like a dark cloud, and they are stuck with the miserable feelings until a wind stirs up to blow the gloom away. Thinking they are helpless, they passively suffer and simply live with the misery or look solely to medication for relief.

In *Take Charge of Your Emotions*, I will demonstrate another way.

Medication is a popular remedy for soothing emotional pain; antidepressants are some of the most commonly prescribed drugs in America. Yet taking medication as the only response to distress does not help sufferers develop competence in overcoming uncomfortable moods. And it's true that all people, at times—whether or not on antidepressants—face emotional challenges. Everyone can benefit from discovering or improving on how to take charge of their emotions. I aim to show how to do just this by capitalizing on three types of relationships:

- relationship between thoughts, feelings, and behaviors
- relationship with Jesus Christ
- relationships with people

As we focus on managing emotions, I will use the terms *emotional health* and *mental health* interchangeably to refer to a state of emotional well-being involving relief from painful moods like depression, anxiety, and anger. Further, although this book teaches skills to overcome painful feelings, it does not argue against antidepressant or anti-anxiety medications. Nor does it endorse ignoring your physician's advice if such treatment has been prescribed for you.

Take Charge of Your Emotions is divided into four parts that build on one another. Parts I, II, and III examine how to capitalize on a particular type of relationship in order to find relief. Part IV puts the first three together.

Part I: Empowered Through Thoughts and Behaviors

Thoughts, feelings, and behaviors are physiologically connected. For instance, how we interpret life strongly affects how we feel, and our actions also regulate our emotions. Though many people fear having a faulty brain that consigns them to a life of depression or anxiety, scientists have discovered that our thoughts and behaviors influence brain chemistry and genetic expression, even impacting whether new cells develop and others die. Taking charge of thoughts and actions changes brain functioning, empowering us to improve our mental health.

For nearly thirty years I have been helping clients take control of their thoughts and behaviors. The method I developed enables people to identify the problem-thinking that creates painful feelings and undesirable conduct, and then turn it around. You can apply the Seven Steps to Changing Feelings and Behavior toward overcoming a single distressing mood, or you can practice this skill daily for a month or more to relieve intense and long-standing emotional pain.

The Seven Steps involve writing, requiring time and effort. Effort itself is essential to "rewiring our brains," according to the internationally renowned neuropsychologist John Arden.[1] Over time, new thoughts and behaviors become automatic.

Writing also facilitates analysis of problem-thinking to a level of detail beyond what we typically can do in our heads. The more detail, the more effective the technique. In addition, writing activates a different part of the brain than thinking, further increasing the potential impact on the mind. Investing time and energy to change our thinking offers emotional rewards.

Capitalizing on the relationship between thoughts, feelings, and behaviors includes taking charge not only of our thinking but also our actions. What we do affects what we feel, so changing problem behaviors offers another path to emotional relief. Helping to build a house with Habitat for Humanity, for example, is likely to provide more satisfaction and joy than sitting home alone day after day watching TV.

The Seven Steps are a psychological tool that appears throughout the rest of the book. *If you prefer to postpone learning this more technical skill, you could skip chapter 2 for now and jump ahead to part II,* which explores the impact of choosing a particular guide for our thoughts and behaviors.

Part II: Empowered Through Jesus Christ

Who shapes your worldview? What guides your thinking as you encounter life each day? Selecting a guide for thinking and living is a very individual decision—it's up to every single person to decide.

The Christian faith asserts that God exists, that he created the universe, and that he came to earth in the person of Jesus, in part to offer himself as guide to everyone. *Take Charge of*

Your Emotions accepts these claims as truth, and part II explores how a relationship with Christ provides a solid foundation for emotional health. It enhances well-being by delivering comfort and confidence that penetrate and permeate the soul, guidance on avoiding traps that lead to misery, and hope in the face of life's many challenges.

Part III: Empowered Through People

Humans are social beings who suffer emotionally when alienated from self or others. We can enhance our mental health by improving relationships with people, starting with the self. Strong friendships with others are high priorities for many, but how intentional are you about building a satisfying relationship with yourself? No matter how busy life may be, at times the pace slows and we must look in the mirror. If we don't like what we see, such feelings as insecurity and discontentment arise; as they impact thoughts and behaviors both toward ourselves and toward others, emotional health suffers. Part III presents practical ideas for building a satisfying relationship with self, then exposes barriers to building friendships and offers strategies to enrich connections with others.

Part IV: Taking Charge of Your Emotions

The final section integrates all the relationships considered in the book's first three parts as a prescription for emotional health. Part IV, which includes chapters on depression, anxiety, and anger, shows how to utilize these relationships to overcome mental anguish and find relief, and closes by exploring how they bring us joy.

Who can benefit from reading this book and practicing its strategies? Nearly everyone. Whether you are challenged with severe depression and anxiety, with frequent temper flares, or merely with an occasional unwelcome mood—whatever your emotional makeup, you can become better equipped, and you can improve your mental health.

The groundwork is laid. Get ready to take charge!

PART I

EMPOWERED THROUGH THOUGHTS *and* BEHAVIORS

1

Connecting Self-Talk, Feelings, and Behaviors

Reed feels like a robot, merely going through life's motions. Nothing interests him. Nothing excites him. Nothing brings him joy. His wife is his only friend, but over their twenty-year marriage they have drifted apart and now invest little in their relationship. He hardly knows his two children; his usual conversation starter "How are your grades?" rarely elicits more than "Fine" in response.

For Reed, every task appears daunting. His job seems meaningless. He finds it difficult to muster enough energy to go to work each morning, and even more challenging to deal with his family when he gets home in the afternoon. What he most looks forward to each day is bedtime, for sleep is his only relief from the constant hovering gloom.

Reed simply exists, neither expecting nor receiving much from life. Depression dominates him.

Mattie lives in dread of making mistakes. She spends agonizing hours reliving blunders, beating herself up for yesterday's ill-timed or insensitive comment, regretting decisions that did not yield the desired results. When for a time she is done reviewing the past, she hones in on the future, stymied by the available choices, afraid to select an option for fear of missing the best one.

Mattie cannot risk failure, so she undertakes only what she knows she can do well, significantly limiting her experiences and opportunities for growth. And her primary goal of avoiding any misstep isolates her from other people. She never initiates a social gathering due to worries that the venue or activity she would suggest might disappoint. Unwilling to take responsibility for choices involving family or friends, Mattie waits for others to reach out and make the decisions.

Mattie is bound up with fear, the tyrannical emotion that dictates her life.

Nora wishes people around her would quit being so irritating. She is set off by the smallest annoyance. People regularly fail to meet her expectations, and this exasperates her no end.

Although she usually spouts off when mad, sometimes Nora simply shuts down and disengages. She feels used by her husband and three children, unappreciated for how hard she works at home and at her job in sales. It seems everyone not only places demands on her but also tries to control her.

Nora is wound tight with anger.

Reed, Mattie, and Nora[1] have something in common: they are at the mercy of their emotions. They have something else in common as well: none of them needs to stay there. Let's begin by examining how to capitalize on the relationship between thoughts, feelings, and behavior.

Each of us constantly interprets life. We all observe what's happening and carry on an internal dialogue about what we see or, more broadly, what we sense and intuit. This continuous and often automatic inner conversation, or self-talk, is something like the play-by-play during a football game. When Nora encounters a traffic jam, she does not ask, "What should I tell myself about this traffic?" but rather, in her case, says or thinks, "I don't have time for this" or "I'm sick to death of gridlock!"

Through the years, Nora has developed habitual ways of interpreting situations. She seldom pays attention to her self-talk; she simply lives her life. But whether or not she tunes in to her auto-interpretations, what she tells herself about life around her creates her feelings and behaviors—if the self-talk is believable.

The Problem With "Positive Thinking"

Not every thought impacts our feelings and behaviors. For instance, Nora has heard many people say, "Just think positively." However, when she has an appointment with a client in five minutes, yet is ten miles away and crawling along, wishfully but untruthfully saying "I'm sure I'll make it on time" is useless. She knows it's impossible to travel ten miles in five minutes when the traffic is standing still—it wouldn't even be possible if she drove the whole distance at ninety miles an hour. Interpreting her situation that way neither creates *feelings* of relief nor produces the *behavior* of careful driving.

Nora is by no means the only skeptic about "positive thinking." The issue with positive thinking is that often it's difficult to believe. When Craig sits for his final physics exam, merely telling himself "I know I'll get an A" will not boost his confidence if up to this point he has done C work, for no evidence supports his contention.

Likewise, Brandon's anticipating a blind date with Michelle by saying "There's no way she won't like me" doesn't help much either. He's not a narcissist and, further, he knows from experience that not everyone will desire his company. Similarly, Susan, who spends each dollar she gets and is presently short on cash, will not find much relief from asserting "Payday is tomorrow" when she knows it is actually ten days away. Unless self-talk is fully believable, it has little or no impact on our feelings and behaviors.

Helpful Self-Talk (Instead of "Positive Thinking")

Within the realm of believability are a number of options for how every situation can be interpreted. Nora, barely moving in traffic before her appointment, could tell herself, "If this stupid holdup makes me late I'll lose the contract!" Such *unhelpful self-talk* probably would create feelings of frustration and alarm likely to engender behaviors of tailgating, darting in and out of traffic, and white-knuckling the wheel.

Here's another possible option, just as believable to Nora but resulting in different and more desirable feelings and behaviors:

> It seems I'm going to be late. Getting all worked up won't bring me there any faster. I can call ahead to say I'm stuck in traffic and sincerely apologize. How quickly traffic moves and how my client reacts are out of my control. I might as well sit back and turn on the radio. I will learn from this and leave earlier next time.

This *helpful self-talk* acknowledges the truth ("I'm going to be late") but recognizes the futility of getting bent out of shape. Subsequently, Nora feels more relaxed and drives responsibly. It is unrealistic to think she would feel happy about arriving late, but it is very possible for her to compose herself.

I use the terms *unhelpful* and *helpful* instead of *negative* and *positive* to countermand the overly simplistic notion that thinking positively is all that is necessary to feel good (or feel better). Again, positive thinking that's unbelievable, or not credible, is useless. Conversely, interpreting life in a truthful and helpful way does lead to more desirable feelings and behaviors.

Most people would agree that Craig, taking his physics final, wouldn't foster good results with unhelpful self-talk like "I know I'm going to fail this—I can't do it!" (In fact, it would create feelings of being overwhelmed as well as behaviors like distraction and freezing up.) My point is that thinking and speaking with unrealistic positivity won't produce confidence or improve his focus either; this also is useless. In contrast is helpful self-talk, which will calm him and enhance his concentration: "What's in my control right now is to read one question at a time and do my best. Let go of the outcome."

In the same way, of the many different things Brandon can tell himself about meeting Michelle for the first time, what's sure is that his interpretation of the situation will cultivate his feelings and behaviors. If he tells himself, "She has to like me!" he probably will feel stressed and pressured and probably will try too hard to impress her. The *positive* thought of "There's no doubt she'll like me" is unconvincing when they haven't even met. Much better if he chooses *helpful* self-talk:

> I look forward to spending time with Michelle and getting to know her. She doesn't hold the key to my future happiness—I'm not handing out that kind of power. We're just going to spend a couple of hours together. No big deal.

Brandon's approach promotes feelings of confidence and assurance. Correspondingly, when out with her, he enjoys being himself—acts natural—and is able to focus on learning about her.

Spendthrift Susan, short on cash with a week and a half until her next check, also faces important decisions as to how she will construe her situation. Unhelpful self-talk could be, "I really might not survive till then!" This could generate feelings of fear and behaviors of wheel-spinning. Helpful self-talk, acknowledging the facts, might be,

> I must learn to budget better; I can, and I will. If need be, I'll go to a food shelf to tide me over. I won't starve on a couple weeks of beans and rice; plus, the diet can motivate me to plan ahead in the future and spend my money wisely.

This should spawn feelings of resolve and determination, and behaviors of making a plan, writing a budget, and, perhaps, going to the food shelf.

The Power of Feelings

We have seen examples of how self-talk impacts feelings and behaviors. In addition, our feelings also shape our self-talk and our behaviors.

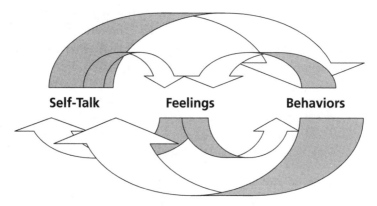

Self-Talk   **Feelings**   **Behaviors**

Each of these three factors powerfully affects the other two. Again, everyone develops automatic ways of interpreting life.

24

However, when people are struggling with a particular emotional challenge, their self-talk often is colored by their mood and becomes a habitual reflection of painful feelings.

For example, depressed people fall into the rut of interpreting life negatively. Reed, recently passed over for a promotion, said, "No surprise they chose someone else. I'm not good at anything." When considering his situation, he regularly tells himself, "Every day it's the same old routine. Life is so boring." And he sees no relief on the horizon, frequently lamenting, "I'll never feel better."

Cognitive psychiatrist Aaron Beck identified what he calls the "cognitive triad of depression,"[2] three beliefs that depressed people tend to hold. They have a negative view of themselves, a negative view of life around them, and a negative view of the future. In other words, they are down on themselves, they feel that little if anything brings them joy, and they don't believe things will improve. Having developed the habit of interpreting life pessimistically, they see themselves as inadequate, life as dull or meaningless, and the future as hopeless.

"Themes of danger" dominate the self-talk of anxious people, according to Beck,[3] who noted that when interpreting life they "maximize the likelihood of harm and minimize their ability to cope."[4] They tell themselves that terrible things are going to happen and that they will fall apart when the horrible events confront them. For instance, in response to her daughter wanting to play soccer, Mattie tells herself, "She's going to get hurt! She'll end up with a head injury from which she'll never recover." Mattie also has intended for years to replace her tattered living room furniture, but she will not decide which couch and chairs to buy: "They won't look right in our home, and we'll be stuck with this major purchase forever." Needing to fly cross-country to attend a conference for work, she insists, "I cannot handle flying. We might hit turbulence—the plane could crash."

Having worked with angry people for years, I've observed that among their ways of interpreting life, the theme of angry self-talk is "It's not fair!" They tend to focus their thinking on how they're getting a raw deal, and the feelings that most often result are victimization and resentment.

Nora's sister has a bigger, more expensive house than she does, and she constantly thinks *Why should* she *have more?* When she got a ticket for driving twenty miles over the speed limit, she told herself, "I haven't been pulled over in more than ten years—I deserve a warning first!" After she wasn't awarded a bonus this year despite working hard for her economically challenged company, she ruminated, "It's wrong that they demand so much from me but don't compensate my efforts."

As mentioned above, feelings don't only impact our self-talk, they also inform our behavior. Actions that follow from anger include blaming others, verbal tirades, emotional detachment (e.g., the silent treatment), sarcasm, and cynicism. Nora makes envious jabs at every turn about how her more affluent sibling gets all the breaks. She lost her cool and cursed at the highway patrolman as he was writing the ticket. She has stayed so mad about the bonus that she goes through the motions at work, barely acknowledging her boss.

Certain behaviors correspond to the feeling of depression as well, including passivity and withdrawal. Depressed people may want to retreat to their beds and pull the shades. When Reed learned he would not be promoted, he determined never again to bother with trying to advance his career. He also ignores his family whenever possible, choosing instead to channel-surf his evenings and weekends away. He does almost nothing to engage with life; lacking energy, he waits to feel better before putting forth any effort.

The characteristic behavior that accompanies anxiety is avoidance. Mattie, terrified her daughter would be injured, refuses to sign her up for a soccer team. She continually postpones purchasing furniture, despite having set aside money years ago for the new couch and chairs. In response to her boss's direction to fly to the conference, she made up an excuse and would not go. The longer she avoids her sources of fear, the more her anxiety grows.

The Behavior Effect

Behaviors influence self-talk and feelings. When Mattie changes course and signs up her daughter to play, her fear diminishes after witnessing her survive a few games. Further, the new behavior transforms self-talk from "She'll have a devastating injury" to "She's having so much fun!" Likewise, Reed engages to communicate with his wife and children and participates in a service project with them, then feels happier; his thoughts also shift from focusing almost entirely on himself to considering other people. When Nora opens up and talks with her boss, she learns more about their company's current fragility. Her self-talk switches to "We all must put forth full effort to help this place succeed. I'm thankful I still have a job." Her feelings subsequently shift from resentful and exploited to grateful and motivated.

Taking Charge of What We Can

Here is a crucial distinction regarding these three facets: While all three affect the other two, only self-talk and behaviors are directly within our control. We can choose how we interpret life, and we can choose what we do.

In contrast, we do not have direct control over our emotions. Reed will not suddenly *feel* happy just because he wants relief.

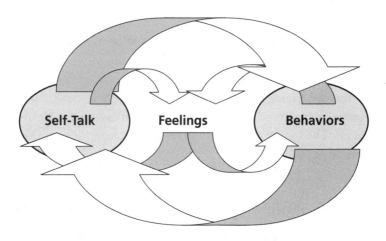

Self-Talk   Feelings   Behaviors

Nor will Mattie's snapping her fingers instantly replace fear of flying with courage. By taking command of their self-talk and their behavior, though, both can indirectly yet powerfully change their feelings. When we make such choices, we begin taking charge of our emotional health. (We'll address engaging in helpful behaviors, so vital to emotional well-being, in parts III and IV.)

In the introduction, I mentioned a tool that has evolved as I've gained more and more insight into using self-talk to transform painful emotions. I call this skill the Seven Steps to Changing Feelings and Behavior, or simply the Seven Steps, and before we move on I want to comment on its practice. People experiencing emotional distress associated with a particular situation might solve the difficulty by addressing it once. (For an example, see chapter 2.) It's been my experience that those struggling with long-standing emotional pain need to spend around thirty minutes daily, or nearly daily, for a month or more with the Steps in order to change automatic unhelpful ways of thinking. This expenditure of time and effort resembles what might be regularly invested in workouts to promote physical health. (Be sure to read appendix B if you decide to devote considerable time to writing the Steps. This section contains many tips that will provide you with more effective results.)

At the beginning of this process, helpful self-talk often remains in a person's mind briefly, maybe only minutes, before unhelpful thinking re-intrudes. As dedicated days and weeks pass, though, helpful thinking sticks longer and becomes more automatic.

Some issues and challenges are so complex, especially at the onset of addressing and tackling them, that writing the Seven Steps will require more than half an hour. In that event, you might consider completing lengthy writings in thirty-minute increments over several days. When utilizing this tool, a key to breaking bad habits in how you think is to exercise your brain nearly daily through writing until your automatic interpretations of life are helpful about 90 percent of the time.

In chapter 2, I will introduce you to the Seven Steps through Tom, a man who used them to turn the tables on difficult emotions. If you prefer to postpone learning this more technical skill, you could jump ahead for now to part II.

TABLE 1

Examples of Relationship Between Feelings, Self-Talk, and Behavior

Feeling	Habitual Self-Talk	Habitual Behavior
Depression	• Focus on gloom • Negative, pessimistic interpretations	Passivity, withdrawal from others, dependency on a few trusted people
Anxiety	• Focus on danger • Frightening interpretations	Avoidance of threatening situations
Anger	• Focus on fairness • Sense of being oft-victimized by injustice	Verbal tirades, emotional detachment, blaming others, sarcasm, cynicism

2

Taking Charge of Self-Talk

Tom felt sick to his stomach as Rick, his boss, closed the staff meeting with an announcement: the entire office was invited to a barbeque next month.

Tom had nothing against his co-workers. His problem was social anxiety. But after four years of manufacturing excuses to stay home, he understood the importance of saying yes this time, even though the mere thought of attending made him sweat. The event would be at Rick's house.

Fear turned to panic that evening when Tom's wife, Sally, reminded him she would be out of town visiting her sister that weekend. Attending with Sally was threatening. Going solo wasn't even a consideration.

With the hope of overcoming his anxiety, he'd previously tried relaxation exercises and positive affirmations, to no relief. And he did not believe he had the stamina to "just white-knuckle it" through this party. Then Sally told him about a new technique that had proved effective for a friend. It required some effort, but the concept was promising.

Sally gave him the work sheet her friend had shared, "Seven Steps to Changing Feelings and Behavior." If this could help, Tom thought, it would be well worth the time and energy. He knew he needed to shake his panic and go to the party. He decided to give the Steps a try.

You can find the work sheet Sally gave Tom in appendix A, which I encourage you to read later. For now, let me demonstrate this process with Tom's story providing the example.

The Seven Steps are based on four key terms: Situation, Self-Talk, Feelings, and Behavior:

Situation	Just the facts of what's happening (e.g., stuck in traffic, sitting in science class, sister is seriously ill, feel angry right now). A situation may be as specific as "My phone was stolen" or as vague as "It's Sunday evening and I feel depressed."
Self-Talk	What we tell ourselves about the facts (or the situation). How we interpret situations—if our interpretation is believable—tremendously impacts how we *feel* and how we *behave*. • Positive self-talk is often unbelievable and therefore has little effect on feelings and behaviors. • Unhelpful self-talk is believable but leads to undesirable feelings and behaviors. • Helpful self-talk is believable and produces emotional relief and healthier behavior. *We can choose what we tell ourselves about our situations.*
Feelings	What we "feel"—our mood or emotions. We do not have direct control over our feelings, but *we can indirectly control feelings by taking charge of our self-talk and our behavior.*
Behavior	What we do; the actions we take. *We can choose how we behave in each situation.*

Next, take out two pieces of paper and draw four columns on each page. Write the defined terms as column headings:

PAGE 1

Situation	Unhelpful Self-Talk	Feelings	Behavior

PAGE 2

Situation	Helpful Self-Talk	Feelings	Behavior

Now you can fill in the columns, using the Seven Steps.

Seven Steps to Changing Feelings and Behavior

Step 1: Describe the Situation

Ask yourself: "What's happening? What am I facing?" Contemplating the barbeque, Tom's first impulse was to write, "I don't want to go to the party!" But that was his interpretation of the event; opinions don't fit in the Situation column. Stick to the facts here. Instead, he wrote, on both pages:

PAGE 1

Situation	Unhelpful Self-Talk	Feelings	Behavior
Considering attending Rick's BBQ alone.			

PAGE 2

Situation	Helpful Self-Talk	Feelings	Behavior
Considering attending Rick's BBQ alone.			

Step 2: Identify Your Feelings

Emotions frequently draw our attention, while the self-talk that creates them can be easy to ignore. Tom, well aware of his aversion to social gatherings, had no idea what he was telling himself about them. In fact, he wasn't convinced he was telling himself anything at all. Step 2 helps uncover subconscious self-talk. (Note: Steps 2–4 will involve writing on page 1.)

Ask yourself, "What am I feeling when I consider this particular situation?" Select words from the Feelings List (below) that describe precisely how you feel when contemplating the situation. Choose between two and six words with dissimilar meanings that represent all of those emotions. Accurate and complete labeling will then enable you to identify the self-talk that is causing your distress. *Panicky, inadequate,* and *vulnerable* fully conveyed how Tom felt about his situation, so he listed those on page 1.

Feelings List

Happy	Sad	Angry	Afraid	Confused
Empowered	Devastated	Furious	Fearful	Bewildered
Motivated	Hopeless	Seething	Panicky	Trapped
Self-Respecting	Sorrowful	Enraged	Scared	Immobilized
Liberated	Depressed	Hostile	Shocked	Directionless
Patient	Apathetic	Vengeful	Overwhelmed	Stagnant
Blessed	Drained	Incensed	Intimidated	Flustered
In Control	Defeated	Abused	Desperate	Baffled
Determined	Exhausted	Manipulated	Frantic	Constricted
Confident	Helpless	Humiliated	Terrified	Troubled
Relieved	Crushed	Sabotaged	Vulnerable	Ambivalent
Pleased	Worthless	Betrayed	Horrified	Awkward
Loved	Ashamed	Repulsed	Petrified	Puzzled
Resolved	Rejected	Rebellious	Appalled	Disorganized
Valued	Humbled	Outraged	Full of Dread	Foggy
Gratified	Empty	Exploited	Tormented	Perplexed
Encouraged	Miserable	Mad	Tense	Hesitant
Optimistic	Distraught	Spiteful	Skeptical	Misunderstood
Invigorated	Unmotivated	Patronized	Apprehensive	Doubtful
Proud	Abandoned	Vindictive	Suspicious	Bothered
Cheerful	Demoralized	Used	Alarmed	Undecided
Assured	Condemned	Insulted	Shaken	Uncomfortable
Excited	Guilty	Ridiculed	Swamped	Uncertain
Grateful	Unwanted	Resentful	Startled	Surprised
Appreciated	Unloved	Disgusted	Guarded	Unsettled
Elated	Degraded	Smothered	Stunned	Unsure
Respected	Pessimistic	Frustrated	Awed	Distracted
Admired	Discarded	Stifled	Reluctant	Embarrassed
Delighted	Disgraced	Offended	Anxious	Stupid
Alive	Disheartened	Victimized	Impatient	Torn
Fulfilled	Despised	Controlled	Shy	Tempted
Tranquil	Disappointed	Deprived	Nervous	
Content	Bored	Annoyed	Unsure	
Relaxed	Inadequate	Agitated	Timid	
Glad	Disenchanted	Irritated	Concerned	
Inspired	Unappreciated	Exasperated	Perplexed	

Happy	Sad	Angry	Afraid	Confused
Satisfied	Discouraged	Harassed	Doubtful	
Peaceful	Hurt	Entitled	Out of Control	
Hopeful	Distressed	Deceived	Powerless	
Fortunate	Lost	Aggravated	Helpless	
Exuberant	Disillusioned	Bitter	Threatened	
Ecstatic	Lonely	Provoked	Pressured	
Terrific	Neglected	Dominated	Insecure	
Jubilant	Isolated	Coerced	Trapped	
Energized	Alienated	Cheated	Incompetent	
Enthusiastic	Regretful	Justified	Upset	
Secure	Resigned	Dismayed	Worried	
		Jealous		

PAGE 1

Situation	Unhelpful Self-Talk	Feelings	Behavior
Considering attending Rick's BBQ alone.		panicky inadequate vulnerable	

Step 3: Uncover the Unhelpful Self-Talk

Now you're ready to write your self-talk. Since emotions are interconnected with inner dialogue, the Feelings words serve as *clues* to help us discover our unhelpful thinking. One at a time, address each word in your Feelings column and ask, "What am I telling myself about my situation that is creating this feeling?" The unhelpful self-talk linked to that feeling will be your response.

Regarding the first word in Tom's column, he asked, "What makes me feel panicky when I consider attending this party?" "I can't handle going" was the thought that came to mind.

PAGE 1

Situation	Unhelpful Self-talk	Feelings	Behavior
Considering attending Rick's BBQ alone.	I can't handle going.	panicky inadequate vulnerable	

Don't use your Feelings-column words here—those are merely for helping to produce clues in uncovering unhelpful thinking. Had Tom used his Feelings words in the self-talk column, he might have stopped, for example, at "I feel panicky, inadequate, and vulnerable when I consider attending the party." Such a statement would reveal nothing about the underlying thoughts that produced each of those feelings. In order to avoid merely stringing the terms together and skimming the surface, ask, "What am I telling myself about my situation that is *creating* each feeling I selected?" Tom first addressed the word *panicky*: "What am I telling myself about going to the party alone that causes me to feel panicky?"

"I can't handle going" begins Tom's unhelpful self-talk, but it doesn't fully explain his feeling of panic. If he stopped here, Tom would be accepting as truth the statement that he cannot face attending the party, and he'd stay home. Remember: in order to defeat problem thinking, we need to expose and challenge our automatic interpretations. Two "power tools"—one a single word, the other a phrase—help us peel away the layers of faulty reasoning and shine the light on our unhelpful self-talk:

- *BECAUSE*, and
- *WHICH IS A PROBLEM BECAUSE* (or *WIAPB*, for short[1]).

BECAUSE, the first power tool, pushes us to get more specific, challenging us to further define or come up with evidence to back our claims. *BECAUSE* compels Tom to identify why he "can't handle going" to the party. Without *BECAUSE*, he could easily accept the notion that he was incapable of tolerating the social gathering. Undesirable feelings and behaviors would then follow: he would feel panicked and stay home.

BECAUSE digs deep; often it reveals that there are no facts to support our unhelpful assumptions. At the very least, *BECAUSE* leads us to uncover specific reasoning that creates problem behaviors or emotions. "*I can't handle going BECAUSE I'd feel stressed*," Tom wrote under Unhelpful Self-Talk. However, he cannot stop here either, for now he must identify *why* he would feel stressed. He needs to use *BECAUSE* repeatedly in order to get to the bottom of his frightening thoughts.

When unraveling your unhelpful self-talk, you may need to do the same. Don't worry about run-on sentences. Tom continued,

> I can't handle going *BECAUSE* I'd feel stressed *BECAUSE I wouldn't know who to talk to BECAUSE I'm not comfortable spending time with my co-workers outside of the office BE-CAUSE I don't know them well.*

BECAUSE compels us to generate specifics to support our claims, but this power tool is sometimes insufficient to uncover all of our unhelpful self-talk. The second, *WHICH IS A PROBLEM BECAUSE (WIAPB)*, guides us to examine *why* our reasoning or the evidence we have uncovered is weak. Problem-thinking is most successfully exposed when we consider using both power tools, asking at the end of each statement, "Which is likely to give me the most interesting information—*BECAUSE* or *WHICH IS A PROBLEM BECAUSE?*" Continue in this manner until you are repeating yourself or the self-talk is revealed as being clearly irrational.

Sometimes *BECAUSE* elicits uninteresting information, providing so much detail that we get stuck in the weeds. If Tom followed his last statement, "I don't know them well" with *BE-CAUSE,* he might write something like, "I haven't taken the time to get to know them." Here, *WHICH IS A PROBLEM BECAUSE* will draw out information more useful in addressing his dilemma of whether or not to attend the work party. Note how he implements whichever power tool gives him the most interesting response until he can see clearly that his thinking has become irrational or he is simply repeating himself.

I can't handle going BECAUSE I'd feel stressed BECAUSE I wouldn't know who to talk to BECAUSE I'm not comfortable spending time with my co-workers outside of the office BECAUSE I don't know them well WHICH IS A PROBLEM BECAUSE (WIAPB) they seem to enjoy each other WIAPB I'll be alone the whole evening BECAUSE people will stick with their friends WIAPB I'll look pathetic WIAPB I'll lose my job BECAUSE I'm not part of the "in crowd."

Tom recognized that now he had arrived at an irrational statement. He was the company's top graphic designer. His job security did not depend on his popularity at the party. The underlying unhelpful self-talk creating his panic was revealed.

Once you have unraveled your problem-thinking to the point that it has become ridiculous or repetitive, start a new paragraph of unhelpful self-talk, addressing the next feeling you selected from the Feelings List in step 2. Tom would uncover the unhelpful self-talk that explained *inadequate*:

I don't have a quick wit and won't know what to talk about WIAPB there will be awkward silences or I'll blurt out something stupid WIAPB people will walk away BECAUSE they'll find me dull WIAPB they'll no longer respect me.

He was beginning to repeat himself so he stopped writing.

Continue in this way, writing one paragraph of unhelpful self-talk for each feeling in your Feelings column. One remained for Tom to explore, and he asked, "What do I tell myself that causes me to feel vulnerable when I consider attending the party?" The following self-talk emerged:

Sally can't come WIAPB I'll have to walk in alone WIAPB I'll be under pressure to quickly find someone to talk to BECAUSE I'll be the focus of everyone's attention until I'm involved in a conversation BECAUSE people always stop and stare at lone individuals entering a social gathering until they blend into the group.

Tom knew his thinking had become ridiculous. He couldn't remember a single time when he had seen a large group of people just stare at a newcomer this way. Again, note how he traded back and forth between *BECAUSE* and *WIAPB*, selecting whichever power tool led him to the most interesting discovery. Through this process, he exposed the thinking that could have prevented him from attending the party. With this same technique, you can uncover the thinking that creates your undesirable feelings and behaviors.

Here is a summary of the instructions for step 3:

KEY POINTS TO REMEMBER WHEN WRITING
UNHELPFUL SELF-TALK

1. Identify the self-talk for each word in the Feelings column, asking, "What am I telling myself about my situation that is creating this feeling?" Avoid using the words you chose for the Feelings column when writing the unhelpful self-talk.

2. Move beyond generalities to specifics. Unhelpful ways of thinking thrive on vague statements that often disintegrate when unraveled and exposed. Two power tools uncover precise problem-thinking:

   • *BECAUSE*: Insert this device at the end of any general statement. It challenges any thought, draws out specifics, and demands that claims be supported with *detailed evidence.*

   • *WHICH IS A PROBLEM BECAUSE (WIAPB)*: This phrase helps reveal *why* the previous statement is problematic.

   Deciding which power tool to use is rather subjective; see appendix B for more detail. For now, first try *BECAUSE* (the default tool) to see if it uncovers important thoughts. Asking, "Which device will give me the most interesting information?" can help with tool selection.

3. Continue digging into problem-thinking with both power tools until you repeat yourself or you see that the thinking is irrational.

PAGE 1

Situation	Unhelpful Self-Talk	Feelings	Behavior
Considering attending Rick's BBQ alone.	I can't handle going *BECAUSE* I'd feel stressed *BECAUSE* I wouldn't know who to talk to *BECAUSE* I'm not comfortable spending time with my co-workers outside of the office *BECAUSE* I don't know them well *which is a problem because* (*WIAPB*) they seem to enjoy each other *WIAPB* I'll be alone the whole evening *BECAUSE* people will stick with their friends *WIAPB* I'll look pathetic *WIAPB* my colleagues will no longer respect me *WIAPB* I'll lose my job *BECAUSE* I'm not part of the "in crowd."	panicky	
	I don't have a quick wit and won't know what to talk about *WIAPB* there will be awkward silences or I'll blurt out something stupid *WIAPB* people will walk away *BECAUSE* they'll find me dull *WIAPB* they'll no longer respect me.	inadequate	
	Sally can't come *WIAPB* I'll have to walk in alone *WIAPB* I'll be under pressure to quickly find someone to talk to *BECAUSE* I'll be the focus of everyone's attention until I'm involved in a conversation *BECAUSE* people always stop and stare at lone individuals entering a social gathering until they blend into the group.	vulnerable	

Step 4: Predict the Behavior

Once you have successfully exposed your problem-thinking using the two power tools, you are ready for the quick step 4. That is to say, you are on your way to becoming your own therapist! To prepare for completing the Behavior column, reread your unhelpful self-talk. Then ask, "What would I *do* if I told myself this? What *action* would follow from this self-talk? What would my *behavior* be?" Tom's answer was simple: "Don't go."

Sometimes people confuse emotions with actions and write words like *insecure* in the Behavior column. Insecurity is a feeling, though, and if Tom *feels* "insecure," the *behavior* that will follow is "stay home from the party." To help distinguish feelings from behaviors, avoid using any of the words from the Feelings List in the Behavior column.

PAGE 1

Situation	Unhelpful Self-Talk	Feelings	Behavior
Considering attending Rick's BBQ alone.	I can't handle going *BECAUSE* I'd feel stressed because I wouldn't know who to talk to *BECAUSE* I'm not comfortable spending time with my co-workers outside of the office *BECAUSE* I don't know them well *which is a problem because* (*WIAPB*) they seem to enjoy each other *WIAPB* I'll be alone the whole evening *BECAUSE* people will stick with their friends *WIAPB* I'll look pathetic *WIAPB* my colleagues will no longer respect me *WIAPB* I'll lose my job *BECAUSE* I'm not part of the "in crowd."	panicky	Don't go.
	I don't have a quick wit and won't know what to talk about *WIAPB* there will be awkward silences or I'll blurt out something stupid *WIAPB* people will walk away *BECAUSE* they'll find me dull *WIAPB* they'll no longer respect me.	inadequate	
	Sally can't come *WIAPB* I'll have to walk in alone *WIAPB* I'll be under pressure to quickly find someone to talk to *BECAUSE* I'll be the focus of everyone's attention until I'm involved in a conversation *BECAUSE* people always stop and stare at lone individuals entering a social gathering until they blend into the group.	vulnerable	

Step 5: Choose Helpful Self-Talk

You are ready to return to page 2 and to write helpful self-talk. The Step-3 exercise of unraveling problem-thinking sometimes gives you a head start, automatically propelling you toward a healthier view of your situation. Writing the *unhelpful* self-talk also provides a road map of what ideas you need to counter to experience emotional relief. Without doing this, the *helpful* self-talk would be only positive statements, which may or may not be relevant to your challenge. General affirmations like "I can do this!" frequently lack the strength to motivate us.

When writing helpful self-talk, do your best to avoid the positive-thinking trap. Remember: no matter how fervently declared, on its own, positive thinking offers nothing if you do not believe it. "I'm so happy I can go to Rick's barbeque alone!" would not convince Tom to accept the invitation—he hates attending parties, especially without his wife. *Helpful self-talk needs to be just as believable as unhelpful self-talk if it is to have the power to change our feelings and our behavior.*

In preparation for step 5, take out your second page, on which you already completed the first column, Situation. Tom's begins:

PAGE 2

Situation	Helpful Self-Talk	Feelings	Behavior
Considering attending Rick's BBQ alone.			

You will need to address every concern identified in your unhelpful self-talk when writing helpful self-talk. Any issue not countered will continue to dominate your emotions and actions. To do this, review your unhelpful self-talk, dealing with one issue at a time.

Tom's unhelpful self-talk included the beliefs that he was an outsider with his peers, that others would exclude him the entire evening, and that his conversational skills were sorely lacking. He was also convinced that his colleagues would lose respect for him and that everyone would stare at him when he arrived alone. It is his helpful self-talk that must nullify each argument that has been feeding his fear.

42

Just as power tools help us to dig deeper when writing un-helpful self-talk (step 3), three others can assist us in refuting undesirable thoughts:

- *PROBLEM-SOLVING*
- *OFFERING EVIDENCE*
- *REFRAMING*

Sometimes writing helpful self-talk involves solving problems posed in unhelpful self-talk. Tom selected this tool first and found he could solve "I wouldn't know who to talk to" with "Jack, Sid, and Maria are consistently friendly. I can seek them out." He chose *problem-solving* again to counter conversational fears, noting that "most people like to talk about themselves. I can ask about their families, vacation plans, or favorite sports teams."

Problem-solving may not adequately address all the issues you have uncovered. A second power tool, *offering evidence*, involves providing specific facts to challenge unhelpful self-talk. Tom applied it to refute the sense that he was an outsider: "While a few of my colleagues talk about getting together outside of work, I've observed nothing to indicate that the entire office is one tight social group." Evidence also eased his fear of visiting with co-workers at the party: "I've been with this organization five years, so my peers are not strangers to me." He likewise offered evidence to remove his dread of appearing pathetically alone that night, to the detriment of his job:

> I can't imagine [Jack, Sid, and Maria] excluding me at the party. . . . In the highly unlikely event that I'm rebuffed the entire evening, my career won't be in jeopardy. Each year at my review I'm told I'm the top graphic designer at the company. Impress-ing others with my social skills at the barbeque is irrelevant to my work product and is therefore irrelevant to my job security.

Tom quickly recognized the value of evidence and decided to continue utilizing it awhile. He used evidence to counter his fear of verbal blunders: "Everyone has said something stupid at least once in their life, so it won't be a new event for the group if I mess up." Evidence minimized his fear of arriving alone as well. Many had been invited, and he knew that several in his office were single, so he noted, "A number of my co-workers are unattached, so most likely I won't be the only one arriving alone."

The third power tool for identifying helpful self-talk, *reframing,* involves simply viewing the situation from a different perspective. This alternative interpretation produces more desirable feelings and behaviors. By reframing, Tom further diminished his dread of attention and fear of looking foolish:

> *I doubt my entrance will so fascinate others that they'll stop to stare at me. If they do stare and find me pathetic as I look for someone to visit with, so be it. What others think of me is their privilege, just as what I think of them is mine. Attending this party alone is an opportunity to get to know my co-workers better and start tackling this anxiety that has crippled me for so many years.*

Finally, he reframed "I don't have a quick wit" with "I wasn't hired as entertainment for the evening."

The following instructions summarize step 5.

KEY POINTS TO REMEMBER WHEN WRITING HELPFUL SELF-TALK

1. Helpful self-talk needs to be believable, not just positive.

2. Every concern from the unhelpful self-talk must be addressed in the helpful self-talk. Fully unraveled unhelpful self-talk will sometimes point you toward helpful interpretations.

3. Use the following power tools to turn around unhelpful self-talk:

- *PROBLEM-SOLVING*: Identify a specific plan to alleviate a concern uncovered in unhelpful self-talk.

- *OFFERING EVIDENCE*: Provide facts to refute arguments set forth in unhelpful self-talk.

- *REFRAMING*: Interpret the situation in a more optimistic way while remaining equally believable (e.g., "the cup half empty" can be reframed as "the cup half full").

PAGE 2

Situation	Helpful Self-Talk	Feelings	Behavior
Considering attending Rick's BBQ alone.	While a few of my colleagues talk about getting together outside of work, I've observed nothing to indicate that the entire office is one tight social group. I've been with this organization five years so my peers are not strangers to me. Jack, Sid, and Maria are consistently friendly, and I can't imagine them excluding me at the party. I can seek them out. In the highly unlikely event that I'm rebuffed the entire evening, my career won't be in jeopardy. Each year at my review I'm told I'm the top graphic designer at the company. Impressing others with my social skills at the barbeque is irrelevant to my work product and is therefore irrelevant to my job security.		
	I wasn't hired as entertainment for the evening, so I don't have to try to be funny. Most people like to talk about themselves. I can ask about their families, vacation plans, or favorite sports teams. Everyone has said something stupid at least once in their life, so it won't be a new event for the group if I mess up.		
	Although I'd prefer to go with Sally, it's time I develop the confidence to venture out on my own. A number of my co-workers are unattached, so most likely I won't be the only one arriving alone. I doubt my entrance will so fascinate others that they'll stop to stare. If they do stare and find me pathetic as I look for someone to visit with, so be it. What others think of me is their privilege, just as what I think of them is mine. Attending this party alone is an opportunity to get to know my co-workers better and start tackling this anxiety that has crippled me for so many years. I'm accepting the invitation.		

45

Step 6: Select the Feelings

Once problem-thinking is disarmed with helpful self-talk, you are ready for step 6. First, review what you wrote for step 5. Then ask, "What feelings are created by this helpful self-talk?" Refer to the words listed in the "Happy" column on the Feelings List, identifying the precise emotions produced by your helpful thinking.

Tom's helpful self-talk produced *empowered, liberated,* and *determined*—feelings quite different from *panicky, inadequate,* and *vulnerable,* which accompanied his unhelpful self-talk. By changing what he told himself about attending alone to something more useful and equally believable, he took charge of his emotions and overrode troublesome feelings. *You can too!*

PAGE 2

Situation	Helpful Self-Talk	Feelings	Behavior
Considering attending Rick's BBQ alone.	While a few of my colleagues talk about getting together outside of work, I've observed nothing to indicate that the entire office is one tight social group. I've been with this organization five years so my peers are not strangers to me. Jack, Sid, and Maria are consistently friendly, and I can't imagine them excluding me at the party. I can seek them out. In the highly unlikely event that I'm rebuffed the entire evening, my career won't be in jeopardy. Each year at my review I'm told I'm the top graphic designer at the company. Impressing others with my social skills at the barbeque is irrelevant to my work product and is therefore irrelevant to my job security.	empowered	
	I wasn't hired as entertainment for the evening, so I don't have to try to be funny. Most people like to talk about themselves. I can ask about their families, vacation plans, or favorite sports teams. Everyone has said something stupid at least once in their life, so it won't be a new event for the group if I mess up.	liberated	
	Although I'd prefer to go with Sally, it's time I develop the confidence to venture out on my own. A number of my co-workers are unattached, so most likely I won't be the only one arriving alone. I	determined	

Situation	Helpful Self-Talk	Feelings	Behavior
	doubt my entrance will so fascinate others that they'll stop to stare. If they do stare and find me pathetic as I look for someone to visit with, so be it. What others think of me is their privilege, just as what I think of them is mine. Attending this party alone is an opportunity to get to know my co-workers better and start tackling this anxiety that has crippled me for so many years. I'm accepting the invitation.		

Step 7: Predict the Behavior

At the last of the Seven Steps, you need only identify the action(s) that would result from your helpful self-talk. It can be useful, before completing step 7, to review the action(s) you listed at step 4, then contrast them with the behavior(s) produced here. Sometimes, though not always, the behavior following helpful self-talk is merely the opposite of what corresponds with unhelpful self-talk. Such was the case with Tom, as "Don't go" became "Go."

So to complete the Behavior column, ask, "What will I *do* when I tell myself this helpful self-talk?" It may be that several actions (rather than just one) may follow. Write them in, then congratulate yourself—you have completed the Seven Steps!

PAGE 2

Situation	Helpful Self-Talk	Feelings	Behavior
Considering attending Rick's BBQ alone.	While a few of my colleagues talk about getting together outside of work, I've observed nothing to indicate that the entire office is one tight social group. I've been with this organization five years so my peers are not strangers to me. Jack, Sid, and Maria are consistently friendly, and I can't imagine them excluding me at the party. I can seek them out. In the highly unlikely event that I'm rebuffed the entire evening, my career won't be in jeopardy. Each year at my review I'm told I'm the top graphic designer at the company. Impressing others with my social skills at the barbeque is irrelevant to my	empowered	Go.

Situation	Helpful Self-Talk	Feelings	Behavior
	work product and is therefore irrelevant to my job security.		
	I wasn't hired as entertainment for the evening so I don't have to try to be funny. Most people like to talk about themselves. I can ask about their families, vacation plans, or favorite sports teams. Everyone has said something stupid at least once in their life, so it won't be a new event for the group if I mess up.	liberated	
	Although I'd prefer to go with Sally, it's time I develop the confidence to venture out on my own. A number of my co-workers are unattached, so most likely I won't be the only one arriving alone. I doubt my entrance will so fascinate others that they'll stop to stare. If they do stare and find me pathetic as I look for someone to visit with, so be it. What others think of me is their privilege, just as what I think of them is mine. Attending this party alone is an opportunity to get to know my co-workers better and start tackling this anxiety that has crippled me for so many years. I'm accepting the invitation.	determined	

Tom may have vanquished his fear of attending the party with this single Seven Step exercise. Or he might find that his emotional relief is temporary because some of his previously addressed worries reemerge, or that brand-new concerns about the party pop into his mind. In the latter case, he would need to address his current emotional challenge each day through the Steps until his fear is resolved.

While it is possible to overcome emotional pain associated *with a specific situation* through one Seven Step exercise, recall that *long-standing suffering* usually requires about one month of near-daily writing in order to change habitual interpretations of life and experience relief.

You too can independently recognize and turn around problem-thinking that creates undesirable emotions and conduct. Please do not be discouraged, though, if at first the helpful self-talk and emotional relief only lasts minutes before a re-intrusion of unhelpful thinking, with its corresponding feelings and behavior. Again, our ways of interpreting life are developed to the point of being habitual, and the breaking of habits requires some time and effort.

As I mentioned earlier, if you regularly suffer emotional pain, likely you will need to spend around thirty minutes writing the Seven Steps nearly daily, for a month or more, to change your default thinking. Then, as days and weeks pass, helpful self-talk will tend to remain longer in your mind as your automatic unhelpful self-talk is transforming into helpful interpretations. I recommend that you keep writing regularly until you automatically interpret life in a helpful way approximately 90 percent of the time.

When writing daily for an extended period of time, people often become irritated by their unhelpful self-talk and want to skip that part, preferring to focus exclusively on helpful self-talk. However, the former provides the essential road map for what needs to be countered in the latter. Additionally, we *benefit* from the motivation, the boost, that comes from regularly finding the unhelpful self-talk ugly and aversive—in fact, this can serve to propel us in the other direction, toward thinking helpfully with increasing regularity.

After reaching the 90-percent goal, people may utilize their new skills only mentally and actually *write* the Seven Steps sporadically, going days or months or even years without sitting down to use them. Then it's probable that eventually they will experience a single emotional challenge or period of special difficulty when the mental exercise alone does not produce relief. I recommend, at this point, that people resume writing the Steps, some just once to resolve an issue, others regularly, for days or weeks in a row, to correct any bad habits in thinking that have redeveloped.

Do not believe you are alone if you find yourself questioning whether it is worth the effort to write the Steps after mere mental attempts to reverse your thinking prove insufficient or useless. In these instances any of us can become skeptical about taking the time to write. I tend to tell myself, "I already tried them in my head and they didn't help!" Then I have to remind myself, "Practice what you preach." After completing the Steps on paper in detail, I am still surprised by the added potency of the written exercise—of the emotional relief that it creates.

Discipline yourself to write the Seven Steps when practicing them mentally does not ease your suffering. While we cannot completely eradicate emotional pain, this tool provides a means of training our brains to think in a more helpful way most of the time and to cope with singular emotional challenges whenever they arise.

One More Power Tool

WHICH IS IMPORTANT BECAUSE, or *WIIB,*[2] is another power tool that can help uncover problem-thinking when writing unhelpful self-talk at step 3. These words challenge you to consider why your previous statement is important or relevant. Specifically, *WIIB* often uncovers the reasoning we use to self-justify engaging in undesirable behaviors, and in some situations, *WIIB* is *the* implement that reveals our rationalizations for unhealthy actions. Unless we fully expose this reasoning, we will be vulnerable to its subtle influences.

Later (starting with chapter 4), I will offer further explanation and illustration regarding the use of *WIIB.* Additionally, appendix B provides more information on each component of the Seven Steps, plus tips for troubleshooting if you run into difficulties when writing them.

Summary: The Seven Steps to Changing Feelings and Behavior

Steps	Self Questions	Special Instructions	Power Tools
1. Describe the Situation	"What is my situation?" "What am I facing?"	Avoid your interpretation of the situation. Write the facts.	
2. Identify Your Feelings	"What am I feeling in this situation?"	Choose two to six words from the Feelings List (with different connotations) that describe how you feel.	
3. Uncover the Unhelpful Self-Talk	"What am I telling myself about my situation that is creating this feeling?"	Identify the self-talk that explains each feeling from step 2. Avoid using the actual Feelings column words.	• Because • Which is a problem because (*WIAPB*) • Which is important because (*WIIB*) Use them to dig under general statements until: • you are repeating yourself, or • you see the thinking is irrational.
4. Predict the Behavior	"What would I do in response to this unhelpful self-talk?"	Write the actions that would follow from it.	
5. Choose Helpful Self-Talk	"How can I change my interpretation of this situation to produce more desirable feelings and behaviors?"	Helpful means believable, not just positive. Be sure to address every concern from unhelpful self-talk.	• Problem-solving • Offering evidence • Reframing • Use them to turn around unhelpful self-talk.
6. Select the Feelings	"What feelings does this helpful self-talk create in me?"	Choose words (from "Happy" column, Feelings List) that describe how you feel.	
7. Predict the Behavior	"What would I do in response to this helpful self-talk?"	Write the actions that will follow.	

PART II

EMPOWERED
THROUGH
JESUS CHRIST

3

Building a Solid Foundation

Praise the LORD, my soul,
and forget not all his benefits.[1]

As you journey through life, what leads you? What powers
your train? There are many different answers people give
to this question, but for each of us there *is* an answer. Here's
one truth we all should know and remember: Either we select
an engine or we acquire one by default.

Some people let *feelings* power their train; in life, experiencing a particular emotion is their primary concern. On that train
the second car in line is self-talk, which leads the behaviors that
comprise the caboose.

"Feelings" engines may drive us toward a desirable emotion.
Sometimes they transport us to wonderful destinations, those
of healthy delight or of inspiration to take action to help others.
Other times feelings engines carry us to places where instant
gratification is the sole focus. Self-talk, the second car, then

permits pleasure-seeking or impulsive actions, which form the caboose. Behaviors on this train might include out-of-control spending, abusing chemicals, continually interrupting people, gossiping about others, snapping or scowling at loved ones, partying instead of studying for finals, engaging in indiscriminate sex, or stealing.

People with feelings engines may also run away from pain. Sometimes this is a wise choice, as when actual danger threatens them. But at other times they scurry to avoid what they honestly need to face. Their self-talk excuses actions that escape emotional discomfort at all costs. Such behaviors may involve not setting limits with children, abandoning important goals if they require sacrificing current pleasures, not speaking out for what is right when others might disagree, or lying to evade consequences.

One last defect with feelings engines is that they sometimes become frozen on their tracks. The self-talk of people who feel immobilized reasons that no action can be taken until depression or another unpleasant emotion dissipates. As a consequence, quite apart from needed times of quiet rest, their passive behaviors might include sitting and waiting for relief and putting off fully engaging with life until feelings improve.

Part I presented the Seven Steps to Changing Feelings and Behavior, which perhaps could be taken to imply that *self-talk* is the best engine for any individual train. But is such a choice optimal for emotional health? Or do we humans benefit, rather, from looking to a higher power to lead us?[2,3]

Part II considers the benefits of choosing Christ for our train's engine, to direct our self-talk, which then informs our behavior, with feelings in the caboose. Solomon wrote,

> Trust in the LORD with all your heart,
> And lean not on your own understanding;
> In all your ways acknowledge Him,
> And He shall direct your paths.[4]

We might also be instructed, "In all your ways acknowledge him, and he shall direct *your thoughts and actions.*" St. Paul, who understood the power of thoughts, advocated submitting them to Christ's control: "Take captive every thought to make it obedient to Christ."[5] Jesus says, "Follow me."[6] The upcoming chapters explore the emotional health implications of doing exactly this.

First, explored here in chapter 3, is the foundation for mental health that Christ provides to those who follow him. Its building blocks are *worth* and *purpose.* A solid sense of self and an indestructible purpose offer emotional stability, even when life is difficult.

Worth and Value Through Christ

In our society, people of all ages fervently seek after self-confidence, and for good reason. A healthy self-image liberates us to discover our full potential and confidently approach meaningful relationships with others. Yet human efforts to create a positive sense of self frequently fall short, for many popular and seemingly potent sources of self-worth are fraught with vulnerabilities.

One such flawed foundation for self-esteem is personal achievement. While exerting tremendous effort to reach a particular goal is often both noble and satisfying, basing self-worth on that accomplishment is unwise on a variety of levels. Tying self-worth to personal success can prevent us from developing valuable talents—for one thing, because we cannot risk failure, an ego-crushing event. Self-esteem based on personal greatness can also discourage people from honestly facing and dealing with their shortcomings. If candid self-appraisal poses too significant a threat to one's sense of confidence, personal growth suffers.

Another common but fragile basis for self-esteem is comparison to others. It is easy to become caught up in measuring our worth by how we seem (or don't seem) to match up to those around us. The biggest drawback to this approach is that regardless of our subjective greatness at any given point in time, eventually our superior will emerge. Even Miss Universe has to give up her crown at the end of the year. Sooner or later, self-esteem dependent on Number One status will be shattered. Comparing ourselves to people in order to feel good about ourselves also sets us up to criticize them; the more flaws we can identify, the more secure we feel. This negative mind-set prevents us from relaxing in who we are and appreciating their gifts.

A third means by which many attempt to acquire self-worth is through approval from others. Like the previous two, this approach appears promising at first but ultimately disappoints all who try it. When we base our worth on others' perception, we give them tremendous power over us. This power transfer may produce a number of undesirable consequences, including constantly fishing for compliments and compromising our standards in order to fit in, which stifles our expression of who we really are.

Kelly is a young woman who sought to feel good about herself through gaining approval from others. Always hoping to fit in, she feared alienating people with her opinions and beliefs, and she shut down whenever discussions touched on anything controversial. No one really knew her because she would not risk stirring the waters. "Will they still accept me if I say what I think?" she wondered. She had many superficial relationships, but her fear of conflict cut her off from deep friendships.

Kelly also is a Christian who wanted to apply her faith to life's difficulties. Familiar with the Seven Steps, she was willing to utilize them when challenged with problem feelings or behaviors. What she was facing now was insecurity.

Observing the unhelpful self-talk and private thoughts of those presented in *Take Charge of Your Emotions* will alert you to common ways of thinking that cause emotional pain. You will see how to unravel such thoughts until they become ridiculous or repetitive and how helpful self-talk then provides a template for turning around problem-thinking toward emotional relief. Notice how Kelly's unhelpful self-talk exposed the thinking that created her timidity:

Situation	Unhelpful Self-Talk	Feelings	Behavior
Having a discussion with friends. Considering whether to share an opposing viewpoint.	I can't express my opinion *BECAUSE* it's different from theirs *which is a problem because* (*WIAPB*) they may get mad *BECAUSE* they don't want to hear opposing views *BECAUSE* this would rock the boat *WIAPB* they may not want to remain my friend *BECAUSE* our friendship can't tolerate different ideas *BECAUSE* good friends agree on everything.	intimidated	Don't share my ideas. Passive.
	They assume I agree *BECAUSE* I can't state what I really think *BECAUSE* they may get mad at me *WIAPB* they don't really know me *BECAUSE* I can't speak my mind *BECAUSE* I may lose their friendship *WIAPB* I'd miss them *WIAPB* I can't survive without them.	isolated	
	I'm not very articulate *BECAUSE* I can't think clearly when under pressure *WIAPB* I may not make my point very well *WIAPB* they may lose respect for me *WIAPB* what others think of me is crucial *BECAUSE* other people determine my self-worth.	insecure	

Anxious not to make waves, Kelly worked diligently to never offend and so "lose her worth." She would not risk rejection, no matter the cost.

Jake, a junior in college, likewise sought approval from others. He continually gave people around him, even complete strangers, power over his self-worth. Rather than shutting down and becoming passive in an effort to please, however, Jake took action—he made sure his behavior duplicated that of his peers. He could not bear the thought of being ridiculed, specifically at campus parties. His self-talk revealed his deep-seated insecurity.

Situation	Unhelpful Self-Talk	Feelings	Behavior
I'm at a party. Everyone else is drinking.	I feel stupid *BECAUSE* people are wondering why I'm not drinking *BECAUSE* I stand out without a beer in my hand *which is a problem because (WIAPB)* I don't want them to think I don't drink *BECAUSE* then they won't want to hang out with me *BECAUSE* they don't enjoy people who don't party with them *WIAPB* I may lose my friends *BECAUSE* I have to drink to be included *BECAUSE* drinking is a prerequisite to membership in my circle of friends.	insecure	Have a beer or two.
	I need a drink to loosen up *BECAUSE* everyone else seems to be having a great time *BECAUSE* they're all laughing at each other's jokes *WIAPB* I'm too uptight to contribute *BECAUSE* I can't connect with anyone here without alcohol *BECAUSE* all my attempts at conversation have fallen flat *BECAUSE* people under the influence are more clever and witty.	awkward	
	It's unrealistic to think I won't drink tonight *BECAUSE* everyone else is drinking *WIAPB* I can't be the only one not drinking *BECAUSE* that's too difficult *BECAUSE* other people determine my choices.	tempted	

Kelly and Jake are not unusual. They strive to find self-esteem through a common means—on the basis of others' approval. Worth based on self and on comparison is no less flimsy. Consider the fragility of these approaches.

TABLE 2

Popular Attempts at Acquiring Self-Esteem

Method	Problem
Convince ourselves we are great, based on our accomplishments and assets.	• We cannot risk failure, so we cannot try new things unless we are certain we will succeed. Therefore, we do not discover our full potential. • Whenever we fall short of our personal standards, our self-esteem suffers. • We avoid honest self-appraisal because we cannot face our shortcomings and thus miss out on personal growth.

Method	Problem
Compare ourselves to those around us, hoping we find ourselves equal or even superior.	• No matter what, eventually someone will emerge who outshines us. Then self-worth is threatened or crushed. • We cannot delight in other people's victories and blessings because they pose a threat to our self-worth.
Receive affirmation and approval from others.	• We're ever vulnerable because others hold the power over our self-worth. • We constantly fish for compliments. • We make poor or even dreadful choices in search of approval. • We cannot freely state our opinions or take a stand for fear we will be rejected.

Worth based on ourselves, on how we compare, or on others' approval leaves us on shaky ground. Worth based on Christ provides a different result. Jesus knows and loves each of us;[7] we are important to him,[8] and he has a plan for our lives,[9] and he will help us through whatever we encounter.[10] Whether or not we accomplish our goals, how we compare to others, and what others think of us cannot destroy or even damage this. That's why Rev. Don Matzat recommends choosing not *self*-esteem but *Christ*-esteem,[11] a rock on which to build self-worth, which is foundational for emotional health.

Some might argue that worth through Christ enables guilt-free laziness, permitting people to decide that since he already values them they need not bother developing and utilizing God-given talents. Anyone adopting such an attitude, however, would demonstrate poor stewardship of the resources entrusted to them and would miss the joy and satisfaction naturally derived from cultivating and sharing their gifts. Choosing worth through Christ lends no excuse for sloth; rather, it supplies a stable and sure source of confidence.

Choosing Christ as our foundation for worth also significantly curtails comparisons. How we supposedly and subjectively "measure up" to other people pales next to his love and care for us and his assurance that we matter (see below, under "Meaning and Purpose Through Christ"). How anyone compares to others is irrelevant. Jesus chose twelve disciples whom he taught and trained to carry on his ministry after he returned to heaven. Some of them received a lot of attention in the Bible, most notably Peter, James, and John. Others receive barely a mention, like Thaddaeus and Bartholomew. Yet Jesus loved and treasured them all. "Number One status" does not define worth. We all can develop our own gifts, confident of our value.

Choosing Christ as her foundation for worth freed Kelly from incessant worries, enabling her to share her ideas and beliefs even when her friends might think differently. She shed her protective barrier and in the process became a more interesting conversationalist and companion. She concluded that only Christ deserves power over her worth. Her helpful self-talk addressed each concern she had identified in her unhelpful self-talk.

Situation	Helpful Self-Talk	Feelings	Behavior
Having a discussion with friends. Considering whether to share an opposing viewpoint.	I have a different opinion on this issue. Being truly authentic doesn't require me to always speak my mind—that doesn't work for anyone. But I also need to remember the potential benefits of sharing my ideas. A differing perspective could liven up the discussion and prompt everyone to more carefully consider the matter. We can learn from divergent viewpoints. I don't have to be rude when expressing what I think. Friendship would be rare and weak if it required agreement on everything.	self-respecting	Share my thoughts in this and/or other discussions. Actively participate in discussion.
	If I never speak my mind, my friends won't know me and I will feel alone. People always risk rejection when sharing opinions. Without any self-revelation, deep friendship is impossible and relationships are dull. I need to at least occasionally express my thoughts, even if we don't always agree. As friends we can also talk about what we have in common. If a friendship ends because I respectfully share a differing conviction, then the relationship wasn't strong. I will be sad, but I will survive.	secure	
	This isn't a debate tournament. I don't have to perfectly state my point. No one is always articulate. I have ideas that I'd like to share. I'll do my	motivated	

Situation	Helpful Self-Talk	Feelings	Behavior
	best. Beyond that, how people respond and what they think is out of my control. They have no power over my self-worth—only Christ can be trusted with that. I'll participate in an invigorating exchange of ideas!		

Jake also tired of handing control over his worth to whoever was around him. He felt like a lemming, ready to step off any cliff the crowd was approaching. Reclaiming the power he had given his classmates, he entrusted his worth instead to Christ and was emboldened by his helpful self-talk.

Situation	Helpful Self-Talk	Feelings	Behavior
I'm at a party. Everyone else is drinking.	I don't need to justify or explain to anyone my decision not to drink. I'm not asking others why they drink; why I don't is no one else's business. What others think of me is their privilege, just as what I think of them is mine. My worth comes from Christ—no one else. There is no shame in having the courage to be different at this gathering. These friendships are extremely fragile if abstaining from alcohol won't be tolerated. I don't pressure my friends not to drink. I will not accept pressure from them to drink. To each his own.	determined	Don't drink. Look for others to talk with. Go home if I can't connect with anyone.
	People, including me, are *less* clever and witty when their mind is affected by alcohol. I won't drink to "loosen up"—using alcohol as a medicine is not wise. I don't have to be the life of the party. I'll look for people who aren't under the influence and talk with them. If I find it impossible to connect with anyone, I'll call it a night and go home.	confident	
	So what if everyone else is drinking? I don't have to. My environment does not determine my behavior. I make my own choices, no matter what's going on around me.	in control	

As Kelly and Jake discovered, self-worth through Christ removes our reliance on approval from others. Certainly this liberation grants no excuse to treat others poorly while reasoning that "what they think of me doesn't matter because Jesus says I'm okay." He instructs us to "do to others as you would have them do to you."[12]

Christians are charged to model their lives after Christ; beyond that, how others view us is out of our control and not our focus. Peer pressure dissolves. Decisions are not made to impress or win acceptance. Compliments are not necessary to reassure us that we are accepted and loved. Christ-esteem stands strong no matter what others think of us, how we compare to others, or even what we think of ourselves. Jesus provides an invincible source of self-worth.

Meaning and Purpose Through Christ

Some people journey through life unaware of any reason for their existence. Their days hold little meaning. Some people place their children, spouse, job, or money at the center of life but then have nothing to live for when a child leaves home, a spouse divorces or dies, a job ends, or assets disappear. They discover their purpose was fragile and sink into despair when it dissolves.

Clear meaning in life carries people over rough roads, but is any purpose indestructible? Christ offers such purpose. He loves everyone, and he instructs his followers to be his hands and feet on earth. Nothing changes this, no matter our situation. Regardless of our job, health, financial resources, or marital status, and whether or not we have children, Jesus desires our company and our help in accomplishing his work on earth each day.

Andrea, a devoted mother, lost sight of this purpose. While parenting her children for twenty-two years, she inadvertently began considering them her sole purpose in living. The day after her youngest left for college, she began sliding into despair. She and her husband, Scott, faced an empty nest; she could not imagine what would fill the void.

The Seven Steps exposed Andrea's fragile purpose.

Situation	Unhelpful Self-Talk	Feelings	Behavior
My youngest left today for college.	I've spent twenty-two years raising kids, and now they're all gone *which is a problem because* (*WIAPB*) I don't know what to do with myself *BECAUSE* I was so involved with their school, sports, and caring for them in numerous ways *WIAPB* now I have nothing to do *BECAUSE* my kids are the center of my life *BECAUSE* they needed so much and I loved giving to them *WIAPB* all I ever wanted was to be a mom *WIAPB* they don't need as much from me anymore, and as of today none of them live at home *WIAPB* there is nothing to fill that emptiness *BECAUSE* no other focus will be as satisfying for me *BECAUSE* nothing can compare to parenting *BECAUSE* life offers nothing else worthwhile.	empty	Passive. Sit around and do nothing except constantly call my kids to check on them.
	I so enjoyed having the kids around *WIAPB* now the house is quiet without them *WIAPB* I will miss their activities and spending time with them *WIAPB* it is so painful not having regular access to them *BECAUSE* only the kids provide me with satisfying relationships.	lonely	
	My best years are behind me now *BECAUSE* the kids are launched *WIAPB* I can't go back to those wonderful days when they were young and we were all together as a family *WIAPB* nothing will ever offer me such satisfaction *BECAUSE* I am familiar with everything life has to offer *WIAPB* it's all downhill from here.	pessimistic	

Writing unraveled Andrea's problem-thinking. With this limited view of life it's no wonder she felt hopeless: a vulnerable purpose set her up for despair. Choosing Christ for meaning in life, however, created hopeful expectation, even with an empty nest.

Situation	Helpful Self-Talk	Feelings	Behavior
My youngest left today for college.	I've spent twenty-two wonderful years raising children, but now they are out of the home. I am thankful they are able to attend college—this is a privilege not to be taken for granted. I can't make time stand still—change is unavoidable. I can grieve the loss, but ultimately I will be miserable if I don't embrace the change and see the good in this. I'm still a mom and play a key role in the lives of my kids. But if I can't be satisfied without them at home, I've made them my sole purpose. That isn't	assured	Pray for God's guidance. Explore other options for purpose in life.

Situation	Helpful Self-Talk	Feelings	Behavior
	healthy for anyone. As a Christian my purpose is to have a relationship with Christ and to do his will. That purpose is always available, no matter my situation, and offers meaning in living. A part of my purpose through Christ has been parenting as best I can, but motherhood isn't the only purpose God has for me. I can pray for God's guidance as I explore other ways in which he can use my talents.		Work on building up my marriage and other friendships.
	I loved having children at home, but Scott and I have focused so much on them that we've often neglected our own relationship. This is an opportunity to revitalize our marriage. We have other friends, as a couple and individually, whom we'll have more time to enjoy. While my relationship with our kids can still be satisfying (perhaps even more so as they grow and mature), it isn't wise for anyone to meet all their social needs through their children.	optimistic	
	It's ridiculous to tell myself my best years are behind me. My life is an adventure with Christ. I welcome his next plan for me!	motivated	

Andrea used self-talk to refocus on Christ, and through writing she identified other opportunities this season in life offered her. Christ is our constant purpose, and within that purpose he designs different ways to utilize our gifts as we live as parents, spouses, teachers, friends. He never runs out of possibilities for our meaning and purpose, whatever our situation.

Paul describes Christ as our "Source, Guide, and Goal."[13] Those three words succinctly and profoundly summarize the solid foundation he provides for our mental health. Jesus Christ, our *Source*, created us, loves us, and provides our worth. He *Guides* our living, and he serves as our ultimate *Goal*—offering us meaning no matter what befalls us.

The all-powerful, unchanging God fills the vacuum inside us, declaring us infinitely valuable, providing meaning through all circumstances. Such unshakable worth and purpose help us maintain emotional stability through any and every challenge.

Respecting Hazard Warnings

Fear the LORD and shun evil.
This will bring health to your body
and nourishment to your bones.[1]

Sin gets a bad rap in our culture. Few absolutes enjoy universal recognition, with "having an open mind" lauded as one of the noblest achievable states. Society often preaches that individuals should never judge one another and, in some circles, judging may be among the worst sins anyone can commit.

Jesus does instruct us to take the plank out of our own eye before we search out the speck in someone else's.[2] But does this mean we must suppress or even lose our ability to determine right from wrong?

In *Soul Searching: Why Psychotherapy Must Promote Moral Responsibility*, Dr. William J. Doherty, professor in the Department of Family Social Science at the University of Minnesota, describes court cases where psychotherapists serving as expert witnesses suspended common sense to avoid judging any behaviors as wrong. He cites the child custody dispute between Mia Farrow and Woody Allen, during which a therapist sanitized Allen's sexual relationship with the daughter of his partner and stepsister of his own children as merely "a reflection of the 'postmodern family.'"[3]

The Stealth Bomber

Is *anything* clearly wrong? In our sophisticated culture, *sin* seems a harsh and archaic word. Belief that Satan exists appears even more nonintellectual and medieval. A more popular conception of the devil might involve a pitchfork-bearing cartoon character with horns, a tail, and a red jumpsuit that covers all but his impish face.

Perhaps this is his design. Who would do his bidding if they actually saw his hideousness? C. S. Lewis, in his preface to *The Screwtape Letters,* said,

> There are two equal and opposite errors into which our race can fall about the devils. One is to disbelieve in their existence. The other is to believe, and to feel an excessive and unhealthy interest in them. They themselves are equally pleased by both errors.[4]

Seeing the devil around every corner makes him too prominent and gives him too much respect. "The devil made me do it!" can also serve conveniently to try avoiding responsibility for our own actions. Yet denying the existence of Satan gives him free rein to operate undetected. Defenses are down as people fail to recognize his ways, falling easily for his schemes.

The Gospels record Satan's attempts to divert Jesus from his purpose on earth and destroy him.[5] The devil tries to divert and destroy us too. The Lewis scholar and professor Peter Kreeft writes that Satan tries "deceiving us with the two false pictures of God's will as joyless and our own as joyful."[6]

The Bible teaches that certain mind-sets and behaviors cause problems in living—they complicate life, bringing unnecessary trouble and grief—and calls this sin. Contrary to Satan's lies, God does not seek to take away our fun when he instructs us to avoid those pitfalls. Rather, with his perfect wisdom and love for us, God knows what threatens us, our relationships with others, and our relationship with him, and he directs us not to go there. God provides hazard warnings that, if we follow, spare us much pain, insecurity, and baggage. As I will demonstrate later, the Seven Steps can assist us in recognizing temptation and help us resist the traps of sin.

So what are some of the hazard warnings offered in the Bible? Consider four of the Ten Commandments and how they protect mental health.

Benefits From the Ten Commandments

The First Commandment says: "I am the LORD your God. . . . You shall have no other gods before me."[7] Some might regard this order as egotistical and narcissistic, benefiting only God. He demands exclusive rights to the Number One spot in our lives forever. How could this facilitate mental health? Other gods certainly compete for power over us. Might not they better serve our emotional needs?

Whatever provides confidence and hope in living is a god. Some people place their confidence and hope in their children or spouse. Others render their body, their physical health, their competence, or even their reputation their god. Education, careers, money, and chemicals become gods too. Why not grant one of these our life's place of prominence? Just as any purpose in life apart from God is fragile, so any other god is fragile too. When they fail, our security dissolves.

Let's consider Adrian's story. He quickly advanced to partner in his law firm, the regional go-to place for business legal services. His wife, Kara, taught high school history. They comfortably paid their monthly expenses, gave a portion to church, saved for their children's college education, and put some aside for retirement. Adrian and Kara selected a financial planner who came highly recommended and grew their nest egg nicely.

Yet Adrian could never relax. He constantly monitored their portfolio, fretting about finances, fearing that someday they would not have enough. Going out for dinner triggered his anxiety. Spending on a vacation was out of the question. Kara wasted little and desired few possessions. But sometimes she craved the freedom to buy some new clothes or even plan a vacation without Adrian throwing a fit. He incessantly controlled, and his family resented him for it. When challenged to write self-talk, he realized his error.

Situation	Unhelpful Self-Talk	Feelings	Behavior
Considering renting a cabin on a lake for a week-long family vacation.	Kara keeps pushing me to agree *BECAUSE* she says we need a vacation *which is a problem because* (*WIAPB*) it will cost a lot *WIAPB* we couldn't put much, if anything, into savings that month *WIAPB* we might need the money later *BECAUSE* we don't know what the future holds, or if one of us could lose our job *BECAUSE* the economy is so bad *WIAPB* we must save all we can *BECAUSE* our future depends on it *BECAUSE* our hope is in our investments.	vulnerable	Don't rent the cabin.
	Kara doesn't understand the importance of saving all we can *BECAUSE* she's willing to spend on nonessentials *WIAPB* she never gives up *BECAUSE* she doesn't understand the need to prepare for the future like I do *WIAPB* I have to put my foot down *BECAUSE* otherwise we may run out of money someday *WIAPB* our confidence in living is in the size of our portfolio.	pressured	
	I end up the bad guy *BECAUSE* Kara's so free with money *WIAPB* the kids see me as stingy *BECAUSE*	resentful	

70

> I always have to hold the reins on spending *WIAPB* Kara puts me in this position *BECAUSE* only I see the importance of not spending wastefully *BECAUSE* our hope for the future is in the size of our portfolio *BECAUSE* money is my god.

Never before conscious of its growing influence over his life, Adrian realized he looked to money for confidence. The money god lavished anxiety on its human subject, as all fragile gods do, and it fostered no harmony in his relationship with his family. Helpful self-talk reminded Adrian of the First Commandment, pointing him to a solid source of security.

Situation	Helpful Self-Talk	Feelings	Behavior
Considering renting a cabin on a lake for a week-long family vacation.	Kara and I live within our means. We don't carry credit card balances. We can afford a cabin for a week. No one knows what the future holds. We could lose one or both jobs. Anyone could run out of money—I don't know that I'd ever think we have enough. Maybe we won't even live to retirement! Being responsible to prepare for the future doesn't mean we must save every penny. Our hope is not in our investments. Money has become my god—big mistake. The First Commandment states: "I am the Lord your God. . . . You shall have no other gods before me." My confidence in living must be in Christ alone. He will help us through whatever we encounter in the future.	liberated relieved	Rent the cabin.
	Kara is on board with saving for our future. The cabin will cost money that could go into savings but that's okay. She's wanted a vacation for years, and she has a point. Before we know it the kids will be out of the house. This will be a special time with them.	grateful	
	Looking to money for my security has alienated me from my wife and kids. I need to model a healthy attitude about money—live within our means, tithe, pay our bills, save for retirement, and, when we can afford it, spend some with joy! I reject the money god. My ultimate security is only *in Christ*.	confident	

Adrian realized he could be responsible with money without hoarding it. He discarded the money god. We naturally cling to whatever we designate as our god. Obeying the First

Commandment protects us from the uncertainty, vulnerability, and anxiety that accompany faith in a fragile god.

The Fourth Commandment safeguards mental health also: "Remember the Sabbath day by keeping it holy. Six days you shall labor and do all your work, but the seventh day is a sabbath to the LORD your God. On it you shall not do any work."[8] Jesus warned against trying to apply this mandate legalistically and taught that "the Sabbath was made for man, not man for the Sabbath";[9] beyond that, honoring a weekly day of rest from our work both stops us in our tracks to focus on God and provides a reprieve from the treadmill of our routine. The self-employed web designer who worked seven days a week in order to keep all potential business tolerated this schedule awhile, but eventually nonstop work wound her so tight she could barely eat or sleep. The Fourth Commandment's value is clear. Observing it helps protect mental and physical health.

The Seventh Commandment also protects our emotional well-being: "You shall not commit adultery."[10] Erica knew a number of people who'd broken this rule and was tempted to join the crowd. She and her husband, Neil, had so focused on raising their children, on running a household, and on their demanding jobs that for years they neglected their relationship. Some time ago she'd begun entertaining thoughts of eventually exiting this loveless union.

Then Erica met Mitch at work. He endured an empty marriage too. At first they just talked business, but over the past month their conversations turned personal. This week they discussed frustrations with their spouses. *A brief fling wouldn't hurt anyone*, she thought. Mitch was willing. Neil need never know. *I deserve a little love and attention*, she argued in her mind.

But this line of reasoning was alien to Erica, and raised red flags. She had never before cheated on her husband, and a nagging conscience gave her no peace whenever she contemplated an affair. Something held her back from acting on her temptation. Finally she employed the Seven Steps to sort out what was going on. To fully uncover her problem-thinking, it turned out that she needed the third power tool, the one that asks why the previous statement was relevant: *which is important because* (*WIIB* for short).

Situation	Unhelpful Self-Talk	Feelings	Behavior
Considering having a fling with Mitch.	Neil and I have grown apart *BECAUSE* we no longer have much in common *which is a problem BECAUSE* (*WIAPB*) I don't see how we could ever reignite the spark *BECAUSE* I haven't been in love with him for a long time *WIAPB* I can't leave him for five years *BECAUSE* our youngest doesn't graduate till then *WIAPB* I deserve love in my life *BECAUSE* I'm a woman and can't be expected to go on like this much longer *BECAUSE* I have a right to happiness too *which is important BECAUSE* (*WIIB*) I shouldn't have to miss out *BECAUSE* I need to please myself no matter what *BECAUSE* life is all about me.	deprived	Have an affair.
	Mitch isn't happy in his marriage either *BECAUSE* he and his wife don't get along *WIIB* Mitch and I understand each other *WIIB* we are happy together *WIIB* we don't get what we need from our spouses *WIAPB* I won't be happy without this fling *BECAUSE* I want it *WIIB* I have a right to please myself.	justified	
	Having a fling could help us stay in our marriages *BECAUSE* we could get our needs met and no one would ever have to find out *BECAUSE* we work together so we could easily keep it from our spouses *WIIB* what they don't know won't hurt them *BECAUSE* neither Mitch nor I is looking to leave now *WIIB* we have the same expectations *WIIB* no one will get hurt *BECAUSE* this is just a little fling *WIIB* everyone's doing it *WIIB* that makes it okay *BECAUSE* my standard for living is what everyone else is doing.	tempted	

Note that if Erica had followed "I have a right to happiness too" with "which is a problem because" (WIAPB), she would have considered why "I have a right to happiness too" is problematic. WIAPB could have led her to the helpful self-talk of "having an affair is cheating on my husband." This then would have propelled her toward more helpful self-talk, such as arguments to counter her temptation and remain faithful.

While Erica clearly needs to identify reasons to resist an affair, they belong in the helpful self-talk. The purpose of writing unhelpful self-talk is to reveal the rationalizations that allow her to comfortably make a bad choice. Failing to expose to the light the tempting thoughts makes her more vulnerable to their harmful influences.

When Erica follows "I have a right to happiness too" with "which is important because" (WIIB), her justification for marital unfaithfulness is laid bare. WIIB draws out the faulty reasoning that sets her up for trouble.

Situation	Unhelpful Self-Talk	Feelings	Behavior
Considering having a fling with Mitch.	I deserve love in my life *BECAUSE* I'm a woman and can't be expected to live like this much longer *BECAUSE* I have a right to happiness too *which is important BECAUSE (WIIB)* I shouldn't have to miss out *BECAUSE* I need to please myself no matter what *BECAUSE* life is all about me.	deprived	

See how self-talk that seemed reasonable when floating around in her mind appeared ugly when put to paper. Erica knew that life involved more than her. WIIB helped her recognize the flimsy rationalizations for breaking her vows. She nearly succumbed to temptation, allowing feelings to power her train, damage her integrity, weaken her conscience, distance her from God, and threaten if not destroy her marriage. Taking her unhelpful self-talk to the ridiculous pointed her in a far better direction.

Situation	Helpful Self-Talk	Feelings	Behavior
Considering having a fling with Mitch.	Neil and I have grown apart. I have been sharing with a man at work what I should be discussing with Neil. Neil and I are in trouble. I will talk with him about the expanding gulf between us and taking action now to save our marriage. I must also shine light on my temptations. Satan works in darkness and secrets to destroy us. I need to be accountable to a trusted female friend and/or Neil for my behavior around Mitch. I chose to marry Neil because I thought he was wonderful. I will work to restore what was great about our relationship. And it's time to get off the entitlement bandwagon. "I deserve" will be eliminated from my vocabulary. Those words set me up to feel justified in taking whatever I think I'm due, no matter what. I took an oath before God and Neil to be faithful—"for better or for worse." This is a "for worse" time. It's unlikely any marriage makes it "until death do us part" without "for worse" times. Grow up and do the right thing.	determined self-respecting more in control	No more sharing personal issues with Mitch. Find another job if I can't keep this boundary. Be accountable to someone regarding Mitch. Work on marriage—get outside help if needed. Read the Bible, pray—seek God's help.
	That Mitch isn't happy in his marriage is a problem he and his wife need to address. It's no business of mine. Mitch and I have spoken intimately with each other and now our emotions are involved. I must immediately establish a clear boundary between us that is no longer crossed—no more personal sharing—only business. If we can't maintain that, I need to find another job. This is serious—so much is at stake for so many people. The one in gravest danger right now is me. I have become comfortable emotionally cheating on my husband and in the process have distanced myself from God. The further I go down this path of deception the more uncomfortable it will be to draw close to Christ. While I still have a conscience and some integrity, I need to flee this destruction. I will turn to God, ask for his help against temptation, be accountable for my actions, and work with Neil; if we need outside help we can see our pastor or a counselor. It will be hard work—not as exciting as a fling. Affairs involve sneaking around in a clandestine relationship. No marriage can compete with that. It's not the real world. If I were married to Mitch, the thrill of his presence would diminish too, eventually. My		

Situation	Helpful Self-Talk	Feelings	Behavior
	guide for living is not what I think would bring me most excitement and happiness in the moment. Feelings are fickle; giving them unchecked power over my behavior is foolish. Sometimes life is tough. True character is revealed in these challenges. This difficulty can serve as a catalyst for me to become stronger and better—to draw closer to God and to Neil.		
	Telling myself an affair could help our marriages is a sly justification for doing wrong. I need to fix my marriage, not cheat on it. Whether we'd get caught is not the issue. I can't hide from myself or God. Cheating would damage my integrity, my relationship with my family, and my relationship with Christ. What "everyone is doing" is irrelevant. Cheating is wrong. The Bible, not other people, is my guide for living.		

The helpful self-talk clarified Erica's need for Christ as her guide. He must be her train's engine, directing her self-talk and her actions. Feelings belong in the caboose. This would not be easy in the short term, but helpful self-talk revealed what she must do—flee temptation, draw close to God, cut ties with Mitch, and rebuild her marriage. Erica, her husband, and her children would all benefit. So would a host of friends and relatives who would also suffer if she continued toward divorce. The Seventh Commandment stopped her from inflicting pain on herself and others. It protects emotional health.

The Tenth Commandment states, "You shall not covet your neighbor's house. You shall not covet your neighbor's wife, or his male or female servant, his ox or donkey, or anything that belongs to your neighbor."[11] Is this command merely designed to stop us from entertaining fantasies about possessing what others have and we do not, or does it also contribute to mental health? Consider the woman so distracted by her desire for her friend's lovely home that she cannot enjoy its beauty. Reflect on the father frustrated that his son is not a football star like his friend's son; covetousness strains his relationship with his son and distances him from his friend. Similarly, note the woman consumed with jealousy because her colleague was awarded the big promotion at work. She quits collaborating with her associate and even contemplates sabotaging her opportunities for success. Envy alienates people from each other and robs them of joy. Honoring the Tenth Commandment offers relief.

Help in Heeding Hazard Warnings

The Ten Commandments and other biblical instructions on sin alert us to trouble and instruct us on how to avoid it. Complying with God's standards safeguards our emotional health. Yet sin lures us with false promises difficult to refuse. A psychological theory helps explain what increases our vulnerability to the devil's wiles and what strengthens us to resist.

The cognitive dissonance theory, developed by psychologist Leon Festinger, states that when we engage in behaviors inconsistent with our beliefs, we experience intellectual discomfort. In order to resolve this mental conflict, or "cognitive dissonance," we either change our beliefs to match our behavior or change our behavior to match our beliefs.

Cognitive Dissonance Theory

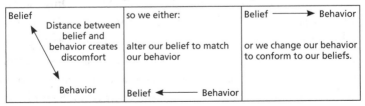

Belief	so we either:	Belief ⟶ Behavior
Distance between belief and behavior creates discomfort	alter our belief to match our behavior	or we change our behavior to conform to our beliefs.
Behavior	Belief ⟵ Behavior	

When we distance ourselves from God, we may more comfortably engage in sinful behaviors. As he fades from our thoughts, our conscience can quiet down, allowing us to lower our standards and make destructive choices with minimal if any guilt. On the other hand, God's Spirit helps us against temptation when we draw close to him and ask for his help. Regular Bible reading and prayer also play a crucial role in opposing evil: "Put on the full armor of God, so that you can take your stand against the devil's schemes,"[12] says Paul. Through the Bible God tells us how to live, creating cognitive dissonance, or healthy guilt, when we stray. This then motivates us to elevate our behaviors to stay in line with our beliefs, protecting our emotional health.

Rescue When We Fall

I once heard a pastor say that if we ever feel we are crouching in a dark corner with someone pointing a condemning finger at us, giving us the message we have blown it so badly our situation is utterly hopeless, that is Satan. The devil aims to isolate and destroy people, threatening "This time there's no way out! Your deeds are too shameful to reveal to anyone!"

He lies—his message is a complete perversion. With Christ, spotlights can shine on all mistakes, no matter how ugly or embarrassing. He welcomes us from the corner, always offering full forgiveness and a fresh start.

Paul wrote, "I have the desire to do what is good, but I cannot carry it out. For I do not do the good I want to do, but the evil I do not want to do—this I keep on doing."[13] Only Christ was sinless. Although with his help we can have victories over temptation, as long as we remain on earth we can never be sinless—perfect. Sin not only complicates our lives, it also separates us from God. That is why Jesus suffered and died on the cross. He took on himself all our wrongdoing so we could be forgiven and start over. We need only accept the free gift of his forgiveness; we can never earn this pardon. Paul goes on to proclaim, "There is now no condemnation for those who are in Christ Jesus."[14] Another gift to mental health.

Understanding our imperfections and ever offering forgiveness, Christ provides a way for us to straightforwardly examine our flaws and deal with them. This realization eventually diminished Ella's defensiveness when her husband, Ron, confronted her about her critical, gossiping style. Her first impulse, upon hearing his concern, was to deny the accusations and attack him. But her unhelpful self-talk, with the help of the "which is important because" (WIIB) power tool, exposed her faulty thinking.

Situation	Unhelpful Self-Talk	Feelings	Behavior
Ron told me I need to quit criticizing others.	Ron told me I'm too critical of others *which is a problem because* (*WIAPB*) he's not perfect either *WIAPB* he has no right to criticize me *WIAPB* he thinks he's better than me *BECAUSE* he points out my problems but says nothing about himself *WIAPB* I don't need to listen to him *BECAUSE* my occasional jabs at others are no big deal *BECAUSE* no one's perfect *which is important because* (*WIIB*) I don't need to work on this *BECAUSE* he is unreasonable *WIIB* I don't have to take his feedback.	incensed	Snap at Ron and then don't speak to him for two days. Make no effort to stop criticizing others.
	Ron says my critical talk could hurt my relationships with others *BECAUSE* others don't like to hear that negative talk, and they may wonder if I talk that way about them too *WIAPB* I don't know that I can change *BECAUSE* it's such a habit *WIAPB* there's no sense in trying if I can't succeed completely.	defeated	

See how following "no one's perfect" with WIIB directed Ella to state the relevance of "no one's perfect" to the question of whether she could be overly critical of others.

Situation	Unhelpful Self-Talk	Feelings	Behavior
Ron told me I need to quit criticizing others.	My occasional jabs at others are no big deal *BECAUSE* no one's perfect *WIIB* I don't need to work on this *BECAUSE* he is unreasonable *WIIB* I don't have to take his feedback.	incensed	

WIIB brought to light how Ella justified dismissing her husband's important feedback and continued comfortably gossiping and degrading others. Personal growth, however, required an honest look at her behavior. Christ freed her from her need to defend herself. Remembering this in her helpful self-talk, she squarely faced her wrongdoing and resolved to change.

Situation	Helpful Self-Talk	Feelings	Behavior
Ron told me I need to quit criticizing others.	No one enjoys being confronted. I'm no exception. Yet a basic premise of Christianity is that all people fail. I needn't feel shocked or threatened when Ron sees a problem with me. Through Christ I can start over. I do enjoy discussing people's faults, and that's not good. Ron doesn't claim to be perfect; he admits his mistakes. If he doesn't point out mine, who will? Others don't give me such honest feedback. I need to take this seriously and work on changing.	determined	Look for the good in others. Monitor my speech and stop myself before speaking negatively about others.
	I would benefit from focusing more on what's right and good. I'll feel better, and others will enjoy my company more. I have direct control over what I say and do. I will ask Christ to forgive me for gossiping and request his help to change. I'm a work in progress.	encouraged secure	Ask Christ for forgiveness and help in changing.

By curtailing gossip, Ella might enjoy improved relationships without suffering serious repercussions for her misdeeds. Some sins carry harsh consequences for the duration of one's time on this earth. No matter the severity of this world's penalties for our offenses, though, Jesus grants us forgiveness and reconciliation with him. Focusing on forgiveness through Christ offers us hope in all circumstances, supporting our mental health.

Rather than a rigid set of rules designed to take away our fun, biblical definitions of sin and directives to flee it reveal God's love for us and his concern for our well-being. Chapter 5 examines more mental-health benefits of faith in Christ, including answers to some of life's most difficult challenges.

5

Solving the Unsolvable

You make known to me the path of life;
you will fill me with joy in your presence,
with eternal pleasures at your right hand.[1]

Psychiatrist M. Scott Peck stated in the first sentence of his classic *The Road Less Traveled*, "Life is difficult."[2] Everyone encounters challenges. Some we have nearly complete power to solve. We can write out and follow a plan of action to settle feelings of being overwhelmed when preparing for guests. We can stay up late and work Saturdays to complete a work project on time. Over other difficulties, we have limited influence. Diagnosed with Stage B heart failure, we can watch our diet, and exercise, and follow all medical orders, and so likely have an impact on our prognosis even while we cannot ensure a functioning heart. Still other challenges are completely outside our control. Though we can take steps to prepare for them, we cannot stop earthquakes or tornados from striking.

Letting go of what is beyond our control is useful; focusing on things we cannot change wastes energy. But what is to comfort and strengthen us when we face unsettling uncertainties? The Bible instructs, "Give all your worries and cares to God, for he cares about you."[3] Yet if God does not guarantee us protection from difficulties and dangers—Christians are not immune to bad things happening—then why leave our anxieties with him?

Christ offers three gifts to assist us with life's challenges: his constant presence, strength to get through whatever confronts us, and a certain future no matter what hardships we endure on this earth. Let's consider how these supports empower us to cope with whatever difficulties we must face.

Christ's Constant Presence

Before ascending into heaven, Jesus told his disciples, "Surely I am with you always, to the very end of the age."[4] He promised never to abandon us, no matter what happens in our personal life or the world around us. Regardless of the relational disappointments, losses, or betrayals we encounter, Christ is our dependable, loving, constant companion. Whatever foes and menaces and disasters we face, he faces with us all we confront. As Peter did when beginning to walk on water,[5] it is easy to sink when we take our eyes off Jesus. Keeping our focus on him, not on threatening, unnerving distractions, offers us calm in the midst of life's storms.

Strength for Anything

Christ not only promises to remain with us always, he also pledges to give us the strength to deal with any difficulty and any threat. Paul said, of Christ's response to his request for relief from a particular hardship,

Three times I pleaded with the LORD to take it away from me.
But he said to me, "My grace is sufficient for you, for my power
is made perfect in weakness." Therefore I will boast all the more
gladly about my weaknesses, so that Christ's power may rest on
me. That is why, for Christ's sake, I delight in weaknesses, in
insults, in hardships, in persecutions, in difficulties. For when I
am weak, then I am strong.[6]

Christ never promised his followers trouble-free lives. He
does promise his presence and strength—strength to get through
whatever befalls us.

Consider Helen's challenge. A single mother with three children, Helen lives in a small home and receives minimal child
support from her ex-husband. For the past fifteen years she has
taught fifth grade at a local school, but with her district facing
budgetary crises, she learned last week that her contract will
not be renewed for next year. Teachers throughout the area have
been losing their jobs; her prospects for another teaching position look bleak. Overwhelmed with anxiety about her future,
she used the Seven Steps.

Situation	Unhelpful Self-Talk	Feelings	Behavior
I just lost my job with school cutbacks.	I've been laid off *which is a problem because* (*WIAPB*) I don't know how I'll support my family *BECAUSE* other schools are laying off teachers too *WIAPB* I may not be able to find another teaching job *WIAPB* I have no other job options that will pay as well *WIAPB* we need my current income *BECAUSE* little is left over each month after the mortgage and the other expenses *WIAPB* we may lose the house and have nowhere to live *BECAUSE* we won't be able to afford even a small apart- ment *WIAPB* we could end up in a shelter or on the streets *WIAPB* we wouldn't know where we'd get our next meal or sleep each night *WIAPB* we'd never get out of that downward spiral *BECAUSE* over time I'll never find a way to earn enough money to shelter and feed my family.	anxious	Spin my wheels. Don't take action to find work.

Situation	Unhelpful Self-Talk	Feelings	Behavior
	I can pray for help in this, but that doesn't mean I'll get a good job, or a job at all, *BECAUSE* many faithful Christians have been unemployed or under-employed for years *WIAPB* I need a guarantee that I'll get another good job and won't have to suffer *BECAUSE* I don't have the strength to endure hardship *WIAPB* God won't help me through whatever I must face.	vulnerable	

Helen wanted a guarantee of a comfortable life. She wished she could counter the unhelpful self-talk with "I'll soon find another good job that pays well," but that would be unbelievable positive thinking in the current economy. Within the realm of truth, another interpretation of her situation offered hope.

Situation	Helpful Self-Talk	Feelings	Behavior
I just lost my job with school cutbacks.	Clearly, losing my job is stressful. Life will likely be more difficult, at least in the short term. Though money is already tight, I will take another look at expenses. I can probably find a few more ways to cut spending. I'll apply all around for teaching jobs—an opening might develop. I'll also consider relocating. I'll talk to everyone I know about my unemployment and ask them to keep their ears open for possibilities. I'll research what economic sectors are still hiring and explore potential jobs there too. For now I may need to take any type of honest work to earn income. I will brainstorm my options and my passions. Perhaps I could even start my own business. This challenge may open up new opportunities I'd never have otherwise considered.	encouraged	Pray for God's help. Cut back on spending. Apply to schools throughout the area. Talk to others about employment possibilities.
	I will ask God to help us and to guide me through this process, leading me to a job where I can use my talents fully. I'll do my best to earn enough for our food and shelter. I accept that God doesn't guarantee me work or a financially comfortable future. This is where faith comes in. I need to trust God with my life, even if I don't see security ahead. Christ will never abandon us. He will strengthen us for whatever we must face, no matter how difficult. If we lose our home I could probably afford a small apartment, but even if we end up in a shelter, Christ will be with us and help us through. Job, house, money—these are not my	motivated	Explore job options outside of teaching. Trust God.

Situation	Helpful Self-Talk	Feelings	Behavior
	gods. My confidence is in Christ alone. I'll never quit trying to provide for my family. But even if I never financially climb back and always struggle to get by, Christ will be with us. I can always find meaning and purpose through him. He can use me each day; he will be my companion and my strength each day. He will bring me through this challenge.	empowered	

At this point, Helen didn't know if someday she would be thankful for the layoff because it caused her to seek and find an even more satisfying career, or if she would struggle all her days to keep a roof over her head. She knew at times in the days ahead fear would confront her. Yet she resolved when writing the helpful self-talk to focus on Christ for her strength and confidence. As time passes, if she stays unemployed, she may sense the need to address her job status repeatedly through writing the Steps. This would help keep her thoughts in check and remind her that Christ holds on to her and guides her as she navigates this challenge over which she has limited control.

Assurance of the Future

How much do you think about heaven? What do you envision heaven to be like? Do you picture a boring place where disembodied spirits serenely and aimlessly float through clouds for all eternity?

God originally planned for people to live joyfully forever on this earth he created. All truth, love, beauty, creativity—*everything* good—comes from him. While the Bible does not precisely describe all the wonder of heaven, it is not silent on the subject. From its passages, the Catholic theologian and professor Peter Kreeft postulates that "heaven is not the mere presence of earthly things, nor the mere absence of earthly things, but the transformation of earthly things. Earth is neither continued nor removed but . . . taken up, perfected, and consummated."[7] The Protestant pastor and teacher Randy Alcorn concludes from his study that "the earth will be raised to new life in the same way our bodies will be raised to new life;"[8] that God will someday restore and perfect this very planet for his people's eternal home.

The Bible offers us glimpses of what our resurrected bodies will look like as well. When Jesus rose from the dead, the disciples saw his resurrected body. Recognizing their fear that he was an apparition, Jesus said to them, "Look at my hands and my feet. It is I myself! Touch me and see; a ghost does not have flesh and bones, as you see I have."[9] After he returns, all Christians will have resurrected bodies like his.[10] We will not spend eternity wandering aimlessly through clouds as ghosts.

Imagine being totally free of fear, sadness, danger, deprivation, pain, loss, and death. Contemplate experiencing God's creativity unleashed and living forever in joy beyond anything this present life holds. These descriptors only begin to portray heaven's splendor. Thinking of its joys, it's possible even for despairing Christians to want to take their lives, with the hope of escaping current pain and entering heaven early. Suicide is not an option, however, for it is not pleasing to God.

This we can know for certain: Jesus offers all people on earth a life with a purpose that he wants us to fulfill, no matter our circumstances. To all who believe in him, he has promised eternity in heaven when our time here is done. Regardless of what we confront on earth, Christians have a "happy never-ending ending" to their story. We will be forever with Jesus Christ in a place of complete joy.

How does this guarantee impact emotional health?

Dane was a competent executive who took charge of situations, both at work and at home. Being in control helped him feel secure. His sense of control was shaken on 9/11, however, and thereafter news of terrorist attacks around the world unnerved him. Terrorists have no army that can be identified, fought, and defeated. They try instead to blend in with surroundings and threaten to strike practically anywhere at any time. Dane refused to let threats limit his choices, but still he wanted freedom from nagging unease. He used the Seven Steps to uncover the thinking that created his fear. While writing he discovered three particular concerns, so he numbered them and unraveled each until it became ridiculous.

Situation	Unhelpful Self-Talk	Feelings	Behavior
Thinking about risks of terrorism.	Our world isn't safe *BECAUSE* we never know where the next strike may be *which is a problem BECAUSE (WIAPB)* now I carefully monitor my surroundings when flying, going to a sporting event, or attending other large gatherings *BECAUSE* they could be targets *WIAPB* I need to protect my family *WIAPB* I can't guarantee their safety *BECAUSE* (1) any of us could suffer an injury from which we'd never fully recover, (2) one of us could be killed, or (3) we all could be killed *WIAPB*:	vulnerable	When in public, constantly monitor surroundings for threats. Ruminate about terrorist activity.
	(1) a disabled person's quality of life is greatly diminished *BECAUSE* he/she likely is unable to participate in or enjoy some of life's best things *WIAPB* if this happened it'd be difficult to adjust *WIAPB* we couldn't handle or accommodate this *BECAUSE* no resources are available to help and God would abandon us.		
	(2) if one of us is killed we'll be separated from each other *WIAPB* the surviving family members wouldn't be able to cope *BECAUSE* they'd so miss the departed loved one *WIAPB* they'd be very sad for a long time *WIAPB* they'd never again experience joy *BECAUSE* their lives would be empty *BECAUSE* on this earth we have no purpose apart from each other.		
	(3) it would be terrible if all of us are killed *BECAUSE* it would be the end of our lives on earth *WIAPB* we'd never see each other again *BECAUSE* this life is all there is.		
	I'm tired of this oppressive atmosphere *BECAUSE* the news is always reporting more plots or attacks *WIAPB* this will never end *WIAPB* I can't handle uncertainty *BECAUSE* I need certainty that my family won't suffer *BECAUSE* only then can I live boldly	troubled	

Situation	Unhelpful Self-Talk	Feelings	Behavior
	BECAUSE my confidence is in their health and safety.		

Dane wanted permanent guarantees of safety for his family and himself, but such assurances are not available to anyone in this life. Telling himself that no one would ever harm his family was a positive thought that was likely but not definitely true. Writing his helpful self-talk pointed him beyond wishful thinking for emotional relief.

Situation	Helpful Self-Talk	Feelings	Behavior
Thinking about risks of terrorism.	No one's ever been guaranteed a safe long life on this earth, even before terrorism became so prominent. Truthfully I'm at much greater risk of harm when driving to the airport than on the plane. It is highly unlikely my family or I will ever be injured or killed in a terrorist attack. I can be alert to potential danger, but that need not be my constant focus. I don't have power to ensure that we'll never be victims of such evil. That's okay. I'm not my family's god. Their confidence is not in me. I'll do my best to exercise sound judgment to keep them safe, but beyond that our lives are in God's hands. Nothing in life or death will separate us from him. No matter what happens here, our story's ending is certain.	empowered	Keep eyes open to potential danger, but don't focus on threats. Go on living boldly in Christ.
	If one of us is hurt in an attack, we'd act to do all we could to help rehabilitate him/her. Beyond that, with God's help we would cope with any circumstances. It'd be difficult, but we'd adapt. Deprivation on earth is short-term. There'll be no deprivation in heaven. God will give us the strength for whatever lies ahead right when we need it. Meaning and purpose are always available through Christ, no matter what. He can bring good out of any situation. We would look for that good until this relatively brief stay on earth ends and we enter eternal joy in heaven.	liberated	
	If all of us are killed, we'd instantly enter heaven together. If one or more of us dies and our family suffers separation, it would be short-term. Someday we'll be reunited; we'll remember and recognize each other and remain together forever.	confident	

Situation	Helpful Self-Talk	Feelings	Behavior
	While those on earth would suffer and grieve, God would be with them. They'd never forget the departed, but eventually they'd find some relief as they focus on their purpose in life. No matter our circumstances or feelings, our purpose through Christ makes our days here worthwhile. Our confidence and hope is not in each other—it is in Christ alone.		
	I don't have a long-life-on-earth guarantee, but we are guaranteed strength to endure whatever we must face and, ultimately, eternity with Jesus. That's enough. I will live boldly with Christ as my Guide and Goal. Whatever happens here, I know the happy ending to my story.	blessed	

Through Christ, Dane could cope with any challenge this world presented. Rather than focus on possible danger, he would focus on Christ. No matter the hardship he may have to endure temporarily, nothing would separate him from Christ, from today through all eternity.

Seth faced a more imminent threat than terrorism. Two weeks ago his doctor informed him that he had Stage 4 pancreatic cancer. At age forty-three, he did not have long to live, and soon this father of three school-age children could not eat or sleep as anxiety assaulted him on many fronts. The Seven Steps revealed his fears.

Situation	Unhelpful Self-Talk	Feelings	Behavior
I have Stage 4 pancreatic cancer. I likely don't have long to live.	I have terminal cancer *which is a problem because* (*WIAPB*) I'm most likely going to die *WIAPB* I'm not ready *BECAUSE* there's so much I want to do first *BECAUSE* I want to see my children grow up, meet my grandchildren, travel, and do so many other things *WIAPB* I'll miss out on so much *WIAPB* I won't be here with everyone else *WIAPB* I can't leave my family and friends *BECAUSE* I want to grow old with them *WIAPB* I am going to die. . . .	shaken	Can't sleep. Can't eat. Can't function. Shut down.

Situation	Unhelpful Self-Talk	Feelings	Behavior
	I'm afraid to die *BECAUSE* I've never done it and no one I can talk to has either *WIAPB* it involves the unknown *WIAPB* it's scary *WIAPB* I'll be all by myself *BECAUSE* everyone has to die alone *WIAPB* I can't handle this *BECAUSE* I'm facing the unknown alone. . . .	terrified	Don't talk to family about diagnosis or its implications for us.
	I'll suffer terrible pain in the dying process *BECAUSE* cancer deaths are awful *WIAPB* I don't know how I'll endure the pain *BECAUSE* nothing can help me through this.	full of dread	
	My family needs me *BECAUSE* I love, support, and guide them *WIAPB* I don't know how they'll cope without me *BECAUSE* they depend on me *WIAPB* they'll be on their own when I'm gone *BECAUSE* no one can care for them like I do *WIAPB* they'll suffer *WIAPB* I don't know how they'll endure their suffering *BECAUSE* they'll miss me so much *WIAPB* they may never recover from their loss *BECAUSE* I am their hope.	worried	

Writing this self-talk was grueling for Seth. It bluntly exposed his dread of the ultimate challenge ahead. Note that Seth started repeating himself when unraveling *shaken* and *terrified*. At that point he stopped exploring those feelings and simply wrote: ". . . ." . Most unhelpful self-talk examples thus far have continued until they became absurd, but you can also stop the process when you repeat yourself, finding you simply cannot carry the thought any further.

Having identified his sources of anguish, Seth could now address each worry straightforwardly, not with wishful positive thinking but with truth.

Situation	Helpful Self-Talk	Feelings	Behavior
I have Stage 4 pancreatic cancer. I likely don't have long to live.	I'm very upset by this news. I don't want to die. It's natural and healthy to cling to life on this earth. We need to grieve this news. We can also research options to see if any treatments might offer me more time here. In the big picture, however, everyone has a terminal diagnosis. We're all going to die, whether in two weeks or a hundred	more confident encouraged more peaceful	Research with family options for further treatments. Read what Bible and

Situation	Helpful Self-Talk	Feelings	Behavior
	years. Life on earth is a breath compared to eternity. As a Christian I know where I'm going. Heaven won't be boring—I won't be a spirit floating around ethereally and eternally. God created this earth as the perfect place for us to live, and Jesus said there will be a "new earth." There will be plenty to explore, indescribable beauty to behold, more access to the mind of God, infinite opportunities to learn, and perfect joy—*forever*! The best earth has to offer doesn't compare with the least of heaven. Best of all, I will see God face-to-face—God the Father, God the Son, and God the Spirit. I can't begin to comprehend how amazing it will be.	more relaxed secure	theologians say about heaven. Talk with family about death, the hope of heaven, and how we'll all cope with this.
	It's common to be afraid of death, but I will challenge this fear with the help of Christ's promises and what over five hundred people witnessed after his resurrection. He died and rose. As he lives, so will all who believe in him. I know something of what my resurrected body will be like based on what I know of his. People recognized, touched, and ate with him; he was not a ghost. I'll see and know believing family and friends who've gone before; they'll recognize me. I look forward to being with them. And just think of the talks we'll have, the joy we'll share!		
	I need not fear the actual moment of death; I will *not* die alone. Christ is holding my hand now and will never let me go. I can trust him to carry me through the passage from this life to the next. It's unknown to me but familiar territory to him—he knows where he's taking me, a wonderful place. I'll relax and trust him entirely as my Guide and Goal.		
	This life is all I know, so naturally I want to continue here, growing old in love with my wife, celebrating the lives of my children, someday enjoying grandchildren. Yet all people face separation from those they love; we all will die. We've placed our faith in Jesus, so whoever dies first will experience no sense of deprivation—only utter joy. No one in heaven would choose to return to earth. And Christians remaining on earth are only temporarily separated from those who've gone before. We'll be together for all eternity.		

Situation	Helpful Self-Talk	Feelings	Behavior
	I'm concerned about the physical pain. There are medications to help me; the suffering will be temporary; and Christ will give me the strength I need. I'll take one minute at a time, with him at my side each step of the way. He'll get me through this.		
	We're a close family. I know they'll miss me. They do seek my guidance and support. Yet their confidence in living and hope for a good life is not in me. I'm not their god. God, their true Father, loves them more than I possibly could. I trust him to take care of them. Family and friends will help them as well. They'll have choices on how they respond to my death: they can become angry and pull away from God and others, or they can strengthen their bond with Christ and with those around them, growing through this adversity. What's in my control is to discuss these options and explore with my family healthy ways to respond. God will never abandon them. We'll also someday be reunited for all eternity.		

Of course, Seth and his family will experience times of agonizing grief as they deal with his terminal diagnosis. They will benefit from the support of family, friends, and church, and open communication about their thoughts and feelings. Yet ultimately Christ alone provides hope in this otherwise hopeless situation. Death is not the end. This life, while very precious and significant, is a prelude to the big event. A place of perfect and permanent joy follows.

This side of eternity, Christians suffer along with everyone else, and all people facing tragedy must grieve their loss. (Chapter 8 will address this in more detail.) But no matter what happens here on earth, never-ending joy—guaranteed—awaits all believers. Remaining mindful of this promise can comfort and support us when we face any seemingly unsolvable challenge to emotional or physical health.

EMPOWERED
THROUGH
PEOPLE

6

Learning to Like Who You Are

See what great love the Father has lavished on us, that we should
be called children of God! And that is what we are![1]

Part III calls on the relationships presented in this book's first
two sections—the relationship between thoughts, feelings,
and behaviors, and a relationship with Jesus Christ—to equip
you to take charge of your emotions. Another type of relationship is featured in this section as well. Part III explores how
to enhance emotional health by improving relationships with
people, starting with the self in chapter 6 and then friendships
with others in chapter 7.

How intentional are you about building a satisfying relationship with *you*? While strong friendships with others are often
high priorities, it's not uncommon to neglect or forget to develop
a friendship with ourselves. Whatever the demands on our time,
eventually the pace slows and we must look in the mirror. If we
don't like what we see, insecurity and discontentment arise,

and emotional health suffers. Some people welcome solitude as time free from distractions; others feel restless and lonely when by themselves. Liking who we are involves enjoying our own company. We can take charge of our thoughts and behaviors to enhance this time alone.

Discover Your Strengths

Approaching relationships with others, we usually identify what we enjoy and respect about potential friends. Building a relationship with ourselves begins with the same strategy. If you seldom reflect on your merits, I urge you to do so now. Start with writing down at least fifteen things you like about yourself.

Some people feel uncomfortable with this exercise, considering it arrogant to name personal strengths. Yet imagine that you wrapped a box containing treasures you carefully selected for your son. How would you feel if, when given the package, he just sat with the gift in his lap? What if he never untied the ribbon or opened the lid to discover the contents, much less removed them to use and enjoy? The psalmist acclaims God, declaring, "You created my inmost being; you knit me together in my mother's womb. I praise you because I am fearfully and wonderfully made."[2] God wants us to identify, use, and enjoy what he placed in the package of us. Recognize what he created in you. Write down your personality traits, talents, interests, passions, physical characteristics, and achievements. What do you respect and appreciate about yourself? Table 3 suggests some qualities you might want to consider, listed in no particular order:

TABLE 3
Examples of Positive Attributes

honest	natural leader	strive to have Christ central in my life
reliable	good listener	sensitive to the feelings of others

trustworthy	compassionate	genuinely interested in other people
responsible	good spouse	good conversationalist
hospitable	good parent	fluent in more than one language
wise	good child	good public speaker
friendly	good friend	good sense of humor
kind	contemplative	can laugh at myself
loving	love to learn	good team player
forgiving	many interests	work hard behind the scenes
generous	love to read	well organized
optimistic	good cook/baker	self-disciplined
encouraging	adventurous	willing to try new things
outgoing	love to travel	make healthy food choices
creative	good athlete	good taste in decorating/fashion
artistic	love sports	manage money well
musical	love music	good common sense
intelligent	beautiful eyes	big picture thinker
motivated	nice hair	detail oriented
mechanical	physically fit	logical thinker
handy	good physique	think outside the box

Review your own list occasionally. Thank God for what he created in you, and develop and use the gifts he has given you for a fuller life. You will enjoy your own company more if you do.

Address Your Weaknesses

No one is perfect, and people comfortable with themselves do not constantly deny their imperfections. We need to examine our flaws and decide what to do about them. To accomplish this, first write down what you do not like about yourself. (You need not identify fifteen weaknesses, unless that many issues plague you.) Consulting table 3 could remind you of qualities important to you that you lack. Include those as you record your shortcomings. Next, identify what you can and cannot change about these. Joe, a married father of three, tired of beating himself up over the same issues for years, decided to try this exercise. Table 4 shows his list of personal flaws and also what was in and out of his control to change.

TABLE 4

My Flaws	I = Inside my control O = Outside my control
I don't exercise.	I: Write self-talk to uncover rationalizations for putting off exercise and turn them around. I: Set realistic goals. I: Identify rewards that I take only after achieving my goal. O: There are only twenty-four hours in the day. O: Unexpected interruptions could upset exercise plans.
I'm irritable with my family.	I: Write the Seven Steps to uncover rationalizations for losing my temper and turn them around. I: Set appropriate limits with my kids. I: Use physical exercise to burn off steam. I: Go to bed earlier—get more sleep. I: Eat a healthy diet. I: Read the Bible and pray, asking God's help in keeping my cool. I: Take an anger management class. O: Other people's behavior (my children's behavior not included—I need to take charge of my kids). O: Outside stressors
I can't repair anything around the house.	I: Get a book and/or search online for how-to guidance. I: Hire someone to do the repairs. I: Ask my wife to do the repairs. I: Ask friends or family for help with repairs. I: Don't repair the house right now. O: Our house isn't new; some things are breaking down. O: Friends' or family members' willingness to help O: Hired people's fees for doing repairs

Joe saw what he could do to improve, but the possibility of change did not mean he would automatically choose it. Now, no one will reach perfection, and that's okay. However, some people constantly beat themselves up for their weaknesses while doing nothing to correct them. For example, Dawn might benefit from losing twenty pounds. But if she does not modify her lifestyle, yet still feels guilty every time she eats a treat, she'll experience the worst of both worlds, neither losing weight nor fully enjoying eating.

We are wise to examine each of our flaws, consider what is inside our control to change, and then honestly assess our commitment to sacrifice for our goals. If we choose not to put forth the effort necessary to progress, we may be better off simply accepting the defect. See table 5, where Joe added a C by the shortcomings he would work to change and an A by the one he would accept. Then he underlined the specific strategies he would implement in response to what he discovered and decided.

TABLE 5

My Flaws	I = Inside my control O = Outside my control
I don't exercise. **C**	I: Write self-talk to uncover rationalizations for putting off exercise, and then turn them around. I: Set realistic goals. I: Identify rewards I take only after achieving my goal. O: There are only twenty-four hours in the day. O: Unexpected interruptions could upset exercise plans.
I'm irritable with my family. **C**	I: Write the Seven Steps to uncover rationalizations for losing my temper, and then turn them around. I: Set appropriate limits with my kids. I: Use physical exercise to burn off steam. I: Go to bed earlier—get more sleep. I: Eat a healthy diet. I: Read the Bible and pray, asking God's help in keeping my cool. I: Take an anger management class. O: Other people's behavior (my children's behavior not included—I need to take charge of my kids). O: Outside stressors
I can't repair anything around the house. **A**	I: Get a book and/or search online for how-to guidance. I: Hire someone to do the repairs. I: Ask my wife to do the repairs. I: Ask friends or family for help with repairs. I: Don't repair the house right now. O: Our house isn't new; some things are breaking down. O: Friends' or family members' willingness to help O: Hired people's fees for doing repairs

Joe chose to accept his lack of skills in household repair. He would no longer berate himself over this. His wife was no handier; friends and family were too busy to address the needs of his aging home. Determined to keep it in good repair from now on, free of guilt, he would hire others for fix-ups.

One flaw Joe decided to change was his failure to exercise. Six months ago they had purchased a treadmill, now collecting dust in the basement. He originally intended to get up daily at six and walk thirty minutes. Instead, he repeatedly hit the alarm's snooze button until he had no choice but to pull himself up and start his day. Table 5 reveals his choice to write self-talk to bolster his resolve. Here is what it uncovered.

Situation	Unhelpful Self-Talk	Feelings	Behavior
It's six o'clock. Alarm just went off. Considering getting up to walk the treadmill.	I can't get up *BECAUSE* I'm so tired *BECAUSE* I didn't get to bed until eleven *BECAUSE* I needed some time to unwind after my busy day *BECAUSE* otherwise I wouldn't be able to fall asleep *which is a problem because* (*WIAPB*) I know I could sleep an extra half hour now *WIAPB* unless I feel rested I can't make myself do what I don't want to do *BECAUSE* I can't control my behavior.	powerless	Stay in bed.
	I don't like walking the treadmill *BECAUSE* it's boring and exhausting *WIAPB* the time drags and I have to push myself *WIAPB* it requires a lot of effort *WIAPB* I shouldn't have to push myself that hard *BECAUSE* good health should be so easy to attain.	unmotivated	
	I've already put off walking for six months *which is important because* (*WIIB*) waiting one more day won't make any difference *BECAUSE* you have to work out consistently for weeks before you benefit *WIIB* I don't have to push right now *BECAUSE* I can do it later or tomorrow *BECAUSE* it'll be easier then *BECAUSE* I've had no trouble in the past following through with that plan.	tempted	

Note how "which is important because" (WIIB) pushed Joe to examine why putting off exercise for the previous six months was pertinent to working out tomorrow. Using WIIB, he uncovered his justification for postponing.

Situation	Unhelpful Self-Talk	Feelings	Behavior
It's six o'clock.	I've already put off walking for six months *WIIB* waiting one more day won't make any difference	tempted	

Situation	Unhelpful Self-Talk	Feelings	Behavior
Alarm just went off. Considering getting up to walk the treadmill.	*BECAUSE* you have to work out consistently for weeks before you benefit *WIIB* I don't have to push right now *BECAUSE* I can do it later or tomorrow *BECAUSE* it'll be easier then *BECAUSE* I've had no trouble in the past following through with that plan.		

Writing self-talk today prepared Joe to recognize the rationalizations that would greet him tomorrow morning. Now he could effectively argue against delaying exercise one more day.

Situation	Helpful Self-Talk	Feelings	Behavior
It's six o'clock. Alarm just went off. Considering getting up to walk the treadmill.	Yes, I'm tired this morning, but I'm tired every morning. The most difficult thing I do each day is get out of bed, yet once I'm up I'm fine. Even if I doze thirty more minutes I'll likely still find it tough to pull myself up. I slept seven hours—that's enough to make it through the day. I can do my best to leave work sooner tonight and go to bed by ten. I'm physically capable of moving my body out of bed anytime I choose, including right now.	empowered	Get up and walk.
	Walking the treadmill isn't my favorite thing, but without much trouble I discipline myself to go to the office each day whether or not I want to. Once I develop a regular rise-and-exercise pattern, this will get easier too. I'll have to tolerate some discomfort if I'm to enjoy physical health. The reward is worth it—I'll get in shape, help my heart, and feel more energetic. Heart disease runs in my family. This is short-term pain for long-term gain. The treadmill is by the TV: I can watch the news as I walk.	determined	
	I've told myself each morning for six months, "I'll start tomorrow" and never followed through. I'm done with that line. Tomorrow is today. Any exercise has value—I'll give my heart and other muscles a workout, get the blood flowing to my brain, and perhaps release endorphins. I've got to start some morning; the benefits will accrue. It doesn't work to exercise in the evening with so many family activities. I'm never going to feel like bounding awake to walk. The time for me is today and now. One-two-three—out of bed!	self-respecting	

This detailed self-talk, somewhat tedious for him to write, equipped Joe to overcome future temptation and realize his goal. Exerting less effort and quickly scribbling some general, encouraging statements about exercise would likely have lacked the potency to produce the same result.

Identifying our strengths and weaknesses and addressing our flaws helps us become more comfortable in our own skin. This does not provide a stable basis for self-worth, however. As we saw in chapter 4, worth based on ourselves, on comparisons to others, or on approval from others is shaky and unstable, sure to disappoint. By contrast, worth through Christ cannot be destroyed. Love yourself because he loved you first—that is the solid foundation on which to build a relationship with yourself.

Choose a Curious Mind

A satisfying relationship with yourself requires not only comfort with who you are but also the ability to enjoy your own company. *Curiosity enriches time spent alone.* No one need complain of boredom. Our world contains endless possibilities to explore, with new discoveries always offering an interesting thought life. New learning also exercises our mind. Research shows that lifelong learning plays a significant role in brain health.[3] Anyone can choose to have a curious mind. If you are not currently engaged in new learning, review the list in table 6 for ideas of what you might pursue. Then devote some time alone to your quest for knowledge.

TABLE 6
Learning Opportunities

- Learn a new sport (e.g., golf, skiing, horseback riding).
- Learn about physical fitness and exercise or lifting weights.

- Study gardening and plant a garden.
- Take a gourmet cooking class.
- Take sculpting or painting lessons.
- Study art history—learn to identify works of art and their creators.
- Read and study poetry—learn about the lives of the authors.
- Learn to play a musical instrument.
- Learn to identify musical composers and their works.
- Learn geography.
- Learn another language.
- Read the Bible and memorize verses.
- Learn about a city, region, or country, and perhaps travel there.
- Study world (or a nation's, or a continent's) history.
- Keep up on current events/become involved in politics.
- Learn to use a computer or hone computer skills.
- Study investments/finances—invest money and track it.
- Study nature—learn to identify and enjoy birds, trees, flowers.
- Take a class through community education or a local college.
- Listen to lectures from The Great Courses or iTunes.
- Learn the constellations—study astronomy.
- Study photography.
- Study archaeology and if possible go on a dig.

Add your own ideas! The key is to continually learn new things.

Observe how Olivia initially resisted this challenge. She spent many free hours out with friends, then turned on her TV the moment she returned to her apartment to watch reality shows. Though often glued to the screen, a vague sense of boredom and dissatisfaction usually accompanied her on the couch.

Several people at work were reading a new world-history bestseller and described it as comprehensive, challenging, and engaging. Olivia had nothing to contribute during lunch break when they occasionally discussed it. She had enjoyed studying history in high school, yet the thought of turning off the TV to read a demanding book did not appeal. Her self-talk revealed her passivity.

Situation	Unhelpful Self-Talk	Feelings	Behavior
Considering reading a new book on world history.	I don't feel like reading this book *BECAUSE* it's long and difficult *which is a problem because* (*WIAPB*) I don't want to put forth that much effort *BECAUSE* it's too much work *WIAPB* I'd prefer to just watch TV *BECAUSE* I want to know what happens to my favorite characters *which is important because* (*WIIB*) it's entertaining *WIIB* I need to be entertained *BECAUSE* it's easy *WIIB* regularly choosing the easiest path leads to the best life.	unmotivated	Don't read. Sit and watch reality TV.
	My life is so dull *BECAUSE* all I do is work, go out with friends, and watch TV *WIAPB* nothing new ever happens to me *WIAPB* I have no power to improve my life.	bored	

Not naturally a curious person, Olivia still could choose to cultivate a curious mind. She could motivate herself to select a new intellectual challenge. Helpful self-talk was the key.

Situation	Helpful Self-Talk	Feelings	Behavior
Considering reading a new book on world history.	Several co-workers have raved about it. I did enjoy history in high school. The book is long, but I could learn a lot. My colleagues certainly are. Reality TV puts my brain to sleep. I have nothing to show for the hours I've devoted to it. What happens to these characters is irrelevant. I'm vicariously living through them and finding life pretty empty once I hit Off. I'll be more interesting to myself and others if I invest in my mind. If I make decisions based on what looks easiest, I'll miss out on great opportunities.	motivated determined	Read.
	My life is dull and not going to become more interesting without effort. I'll benefit from pushing myself a bit. I'll start by choosing to be curious about life. A challenging book will exercise my brain and help develop a more interesting thought life. It will also enable me to join in on the engaging lunchtime discussions.	empowered	

Not all new learning need be "intellectual" (see table 6). Our brains benefit from any fresh challenge. Countless learning opportunities hold the power to invigorate our lives. In the process, they help us like who we are.

Appreciate Your Senses

Helen Keller reminds us of another way to increase satisfaction with time alone: tune in to your senses. In her article "Three Days to See," she advised,

> I who am blind can give one hint to those who see—one admonition to those who would make full use of the gift of sight: Use your eyes as if tomorrow you would be stricken blind. And the same method can be applied to the other senses.[4]

We often neglect gifts we would sorely miss if they were taken from us. When alone and undistracted, we may more easily focus on and appreciate our senses. Go for a walk and smell the fresh air; notice the architecture of buildings, and various shades of green in the trees; feel the wind touching your face, listen to the leaves rustling in the wind or the waves crashing against the shore. Come home and savor dark chocolate melting in your mouth while sipping coffee. Focusing with gratitude on the variety of ways we can experience our world brings new appreciation for time by ourselves.

Plan Time Alone

How do you spend your time alone? Do you sit and watch TV? Do you tackle chores like laundry, housecleaning, mowing the lawn, or paying bills? Contrast your time alone versus time with others. When with others do you see plays or movies, play sports, or go out to eat? We cannot neglect our duties, but if time alone always involves undesirable tasks or passive entertainment, while time with others is usually engaging and interesting, we learn to associate solitude with dissatisfaction. *Liking who you are involves enjoying your own company.* Occasionally choosing pleasant activities for solitary moments helps accomplish this goal. Table 7 suggests just a few options.

TABLE 7

Ideas for Solitary Activities

Hobbies	Woodworking/carving Needlework/knitting Baking/cooking Reading novels, poetry, or nonfiction Camping/backpacking Singing Nature walks Playing a musical instrument Jigsaw puzzles Kite flying Playing a game
Sports	Walking/hiking/running Bicycling Swimming/surfing/windsurfing Fishing/hunting Archery Golf Skiing/snowshoeing/ice skating Canoeing/sailing/boating Bowling Horseback riding
Miscellaneous	Attend a concert/symphony/play/opera. Go to a movie. Take courses through community education or church. Go for a drive in the country. Take in local sightseeing. Attend festivals and fairs. Visit the zoo. Go shopping. Eat at a restaurant or have a picnic. Take a cooking class. Attend a sporting event. Visit a museum or an art gallery. Participate in church activities (worship services, study groups, service projects, social events). Plan a special day-trip or weekend trip. Visit the library/bookstore/coffee shop.
Volunteer Work	Churches/hospitals/schools Political party

Chloe, a single woman, was uncomfortable attending most public events alone. While work, shopping, and church posed no threat, the thought of a play, concert, or sporting event by herself intimidated her. When she wanted to buy tickets for a special event, she went through her list, calling everyone possible, searching for a companion. If no one said yes, she stayed home. Now a production was coming up that she desperately wanted to see. Everyone declined her invitation. She faced a dilemma: stay home again or muster up the courage and go alone. She wrote down her self-talk to take charge of her emotions.

Situation	Unhelpful Self-Talk	Feelings	Behavior
Considering going to the theater alone.	I can't go alone *BECAUSE* people would think I looked pathetic there by myself *BECAUSE* they'd assume I have no friends *BECAUSE* the crowd would notice my situation *BECAUSE* when people attend plays they look around to see if anyone showed up alone, and proceed to disrespect them *which is a problem because (WIAPB)* what strangers think of me determines my worth.	insecure	Stay home.
	I might see someone I know *WIAPB* they'd think I don't have many friends *BECAUSE* they'd assume that anyone relatively popular could find someone to go with them *BECAUSE* most people aren't alone at such events *WIAPB* going alone means I'm flawed *BECAUSE* I can't find someone to go with me *BECAUSE* any relatively popular person could find someone.	ashamed	
	I wouldn't have any fun going alone *BECAUSE* I'd have no one to talk to *WIAPB* people will be visiting with their companions before the play and during intermission *WIAPB* I'd feel awkward standing alone *BECAUSE* others would watch to see how I'd occupy myself during that time *BECAUSE* they'd be fascinated by my solo attendance *BECAUSE* it's very unusual to attend plays alone.	lonely	

It could be argued that Chloe reached the ridiculous when she declared, "Anyone relatively popular could find someone," but since this reflected her beliefs, the statement is not irrational to her, so she continued unraveling her problem-thinking. See her new interpretation of her situation, and how this empowered her to buy a single ticket:

Situation	Helpful Self-Talk	Feelings	Behavior
Considering going to the theater alone.	While I may prefer to attend plays with others, I'm certainly capable of buying a ticket and going on my own. I can still enjoy it. When I'm there with a friend, I don't survey the crowd to spot and look down on people who are there alone. Others will likely hardly notice me, and if they do, so be it. What others think of me is their privilege, as what I think of them is mine. I refuse to give strangers power over my self-worth.	motivated	Go alone.
	If I see someone I know, no problem. It's silly to think a friend would want nothing to do with me because I had the courage to show up solo. I probably wouldn't be the only one there alone; if I were, I could be proud of such confidence. Most people experience times when no one is free to join them. This doesn't reflect on my popularity. I can't control whether friends and acquaintances would agree, but others' take on my popularity is irrelevant. Only Christ establishes my worth.	liberated	
	I'll have more fun at the theater than sitting home alone. Beforehand and during intermission I can read the program or people-watch. I have no reason for shame about being on my own. Those with companions will be occupied with them, not with me. Crowds regularly include some solitary individuals. I'm done missing out when others say no!	self-respecting	

Focusing on Christ

Chapter 3 considered the value of choosing Christ as our source of worth, and as discussed in chapter 5, he is also our constant companion. When alone, we can most easily focus on our relationship with him. A meaningful devotional life—praying and reading the Bible and other devotional material—helps us appreciate and savor solitude. When reading Scripture, recording verses that would speak to you in various experiences or when facing certain challenges gives you access to them later.

Here are some passages that remind me I am never truly alone:

"Have I not commanded you? Be strong and courageous. Do not be afraid; do not be discouraged, for the LORD your God will be with you wherever you go."[5]

You have searched me, LORD,
    and you know me.
You know when I sit and when I rise;
    you perceive my thoughts from afar.
You discern my going out and my lying down;
    you are familiar with all my ways.
Before a word is on my tongue
    you, LORD, know it completely.
You hem me in behind and before,
    and you lay your hand upon me.
Such knowledge is too wonderful for me,
    too lofty for me to attain.
Where can I go from your Spirit?
    Where can I flee from your presence?
If I go up to the heavens, you are there;
    if I make my bed in the depths, you are there.
If I rise on the wings of the dawn,
    if I settle on the far side of the sea,
even there your hand will guide me,
    your right hand will hold me fast.
If I say, "Surely the darkness will hide me
    and the light become night around me,"
even the darkness will not be dark to you;
    the night will shine like the day,
    for darkness is as light to you.[6]

Surely I [Jesus] am with you always, to the very end of the age.[7]

We communicate with God through Bible reading and prayer. He knows our innermost being, he created us, and he will never leave us. Through devotions and prayer, we better know him and what he wants for our lives. This not only helps us like ourselves, it also assists us in relating to others.

7

Building Friendships With Others

A new command I give you: Love one another.
As I have loved you, so you must love one another.[1]

Liking who we are is important to emotional well-being, but we cannot stop there. God fashioned us as social creatures. In fact, solitary confinement is one of the harshest punishments any society can impose. Developing satisfying relationships with others contributes significantly to mental health, and taking charge of our thoughts and behaviors helps equip us to develop strong friendships.

Conversational Skills

A first step in building relationships with others is getting to know them. To do this, we must be able to communicate.[2] Let's consider some basics of the art of verbal exchange, like initiating conversations with people we meet.

Consider William's experience. He shied away from talking with others because when he asked questions, he frequently received short, abrupt responses. Then the ball was back in his court. Awkward silences followed as he struggled to devise another question. All too often his conversations were similar to this interaction with Ken:

> **William:** Hi, Ken. Haven't seen you in a while. Where've you been?
>
> **Ken:** I just returned from a business trip to Chicago.
>
> **William:** Really! Which firm did you visit?
>
> **Ken:** Colson's International.
>
> **William:** (*pause*) Where do you stay when you travel there?
>
> **Ken:** Motel Chicago.
>
> **William:** (*pause*) Do you like their accommodations?
>
> **Ken:** No.
>
> **William:** (*longer pause*) Do you ever have free time on those trips?
>
> **Ken:** Yes.
>
> **William:** (*silence*) Will you go back to Chicago?
>
> **Ken:** Yes.
>
> **William:** (*more silence*) When do you return?
>
> **Ken:** In two weeks.
>
> **William:** (*long pause*) Are you looking forward to that?
>
> **Ken:** Yes.
>
> **William:** Well, have a good time! (*William quickly walks away.*)

William could not end that talk soon enough. The visit was grueling, and though Ken certainly offered no help, "closed-ended" questions were at the root of William's trouble. Such questions play a vital role in conversation—they draw out details. But the problem with them is that they can be answered with few words. Interactions composed entirely of closed-ended questions are stressful, are hard work for the questioner, and require virtually no engagement from the responder. Stilted and uninteresting dialogue results. Closed-ended questions begin with words like:

Are? Is? Which? Do? Will? Who? When? Where? What?

Examples include:

- Are you going to the movie?
- Is this your dog?
- Which coat do you like best?
- Do you play the piano?
- Will you watch football this weekend?
- Who's going with you?
- When do you leave for Atlanta?
- Where were you born?
- What's your favorite color?

Again, while these questions have their place, a conversation composed entirely or mostly of closed-ended questions sounds choppy and unnatural.

In contrast, open-ended questions elicit fuller responses. They work well as follow-ups to closed-ended questions. Natural, more interesting interactions contain a mixture of closed- and open-ended questions. Open-ended questions begin with words like:

How? Why? What?

Note that *what* can begin both closed- and open-ended questions. Examples of the latter include:

- How do you find time to work out, week to week?
- Why did you choose to adopt a beagle rather than another breed?
- What do you think is happening with the economy?

Notice how the conversation changes, and how much more information is shared, when William asks a mixture of question-types. His open-ended questions are italicized.

> **William:** Hi, Ken. Haven't seen you in a while. Where've you been?
>
> **Ken:** I just returned from a business trip to Chicago.
>
> **William:** Really! *What were you working on there?*
>
> **Ken:** We met with a couple potential clients about project proposals. It was two solid days of meetings.
>
> **William:** That sounds intense. Were you satisfied with the outcomes?
>
> **Ken:** Yes, it was a productive trip.
>
> **William:** *How did you end up working for Wales & Donahue?*
>
> **Ken:** I attended a job fair straight out of college. Wales & Donahue had a booth there, and I talked with their recruiters.
>
> **William:** *What sold you on them?*
>
> **Ken:** The work sounded challenging. There were opportunities for advancement too, and I wanted to see the world.
>
> **William:** Where's your favorite place to travel?
>
> **Ken:** Rome.
>
> **William:** *Why Rome?*
>
> **Ken:** I love the history, the food is delicious, and it's a beautiful city.
>
> **William:** I've never left the U.S.—would love to make it there someday.

The open-/closed- combo created a smoother and more naturally flowing dialogue. It also spared William the burden of carrying the conversation.

When talking with others we need to pay attention not only to our words but also to the nonverbal messages we convey. Both communicate emotion and attitude.

Consider first the impact of tone of voice. Imagine a teenage girl saying to her mother, in a sincere manner, "Thanks a lot, Mom." Now picture her repeating these exact words but in a disrespectful, sarcastic manner. Identical words can convey opposite meanings, based entirely on tone. Tone of voice communicates sincerity or sarcasm, warmth or detachment, sadness or joy, respect or disrespect, tension or comfort. It must also be congruent with the issue being discussed. For example, sounding enthusiastic when asking how a friend is coping with her mother's death would not be appropriate.

Body language communicates volumes and needs to be consistent with the subject matter. Eye contact and facial expression are just two ways in which we communicate nonverbally. Looking people in the eyes and a facial expression consistent with the conversation topic contribute significantly to the message we convey. Obviously, tensing my facial muscles to look angry, or completely relaxing them so that I appear bored, does not invite others to tell me about their children. Neither does looking past the other person at a party, searching for different conversation partners.

Good listening skills, vital to positive relationships with others, start with body language, which transmits messages when we speak *and* when we listen. Consider the husband who wouldn't put aside the newspaper when his wife spoke to him. When she protested that he wasn't listening to her, he defended himself with, "I *was* listening—I can repeat back everything you just said!"

This failed to satisfy her. She wanted him to face her and look her in the eyes when they spoke. And she is not alone. Everyone appreciates listeners whose body language conveys respect and interest in what they have to say. Occasional nodding and uttering sounds such as "ah," "uh-huh," or "hmm" when we agree or disagree can indicate we are tracking the speaker's comments, but these are helpful only when we truly pay attention. Those same sounds and nonverbal communications have the opposite effect when employed to pretend we're listening while we're multitasking.

Posture congruent with the speaker's message further demonstrates our involvement in the conversation. Usually not crossing our arms or placing our hands on our hips but having a more open, relaxed posture invites others to share with us. Additionally, leaning forward, rather than slouching, expresses concern if someone is pouring out her heart to us.

Sometimes people exaggerate these nonverbal ways of attending to what they're hearing to mock and intimidate the speaker, discouraging them from seeking undivided attention. Such disrespectful and hostile body language usually shuts down communication and builds barriers between people.

Other body language can discourage people from communicating with us too, as Kelsey demonstrates. She loved to talk. In fact, she could barely contain herself when others spoke, so eager was she to blurt out her next thought. Her excited eyes and fidgety body radiated impatience, silently pushing others to wrap up so she could take the stage once again.

In order for Kelsey to listen well, she needed to put forth a conscious effort to relax her face when her companions spoke. Concentrating on what others are saying and asking good follow-up questions helps them feel heard. She could practice self-control, letting others completely finish their comments before adding her piece. Purposely working not only to contain an impulse to interrupt but also to slow down and take in what another person is saying, contributes to mutually satisfying conversations.

Initiating a Social Life

Prepared to converse, the next component to building friendships is initiating a get-together with others. Many isolated individuals wait for others to call, sitting home months on end with little social interaction. I encourage everyone to take responsibility for initiating 90 percent of their time with others. This can be an intimidating task for some, especially those who fear rejection.

Bridget fell into this category. She remembered Caitlin from high school when they recently crossed paths at the grocery store. Caitlin impressed her as an intriguing and kind individual; Bridget wanted to get to know her better. Yet she feared Caitlin might not welcome an invitation to get together. Her unhelpful self-talk uncovered her dread of rejection.

Situation	Unhelpful Self-Talk	Feelings	Behavior
Considering asking Caitlin to meet for coffee.	Caitlin has never asked me to get together *BECAUSE* she must not desire my company *BECAUSE* if she wanted to spend time with me she would initiate *BECAUSE* all people take action to socialize with anyone they care to get to know.	reluctant	Don't call.
	Caitlin may decline my invitation *BECAUSE* she really isn't interested *which is a problem because (WIAPB)* it would be awkward *BECAUSE* she'd have to come up with some excuse *WIAPB* we'd both know she wasn't interested in my friendship *WIAPB* she'd look down on me *BECAUSE* I reached out to her *WIAPB* what she thinks of me is very important *BECAUSE* Caitlin determines my worth.	insecure	
	I don't know what I'd talk about *BECAUSE* I don't know Caitlin well *WIAPB* there might be awkward silences, or I may talk about things she finds annoying or uninteresting *WIAPB* she may not enjoy our time *WIAPB* she may not want to be my friend *WIAPB* I can't risk her rejection *BECAUSE* if she does reject me then I don't measure up *BECAUSE* Caitlin is the ultimate judge of my worth.	shy	

Bridget's insecurity about her ability to sustain compelling conversation over coffee is a legitimate concern. Though less of a time commitment, this is similar to getting together for dinner.

One of the most common social events but the one that presents the most difficult conversational challenge, dinner offers few built-in topics to discuss, and it carries expectations, especially when first spending time with others, to keep conversation going.

Other activities carry less such demands and include more built-in discussion topics. For example, Bridget could suggest that they attend a play, concert, or movie together. Going out for coffee afterward, she and Caitlin could then share impressions of what they experienced. Going to a sporting event requires more conversation than a movie, but if companions run out of ideas of what to discuss while there, they can comfortably watch the game, which itself also supplies built-in topics for comment.

After considering her options, Bridget stuck with her original plan and extended an invite for coffee. She wanted to learn about what was happening in Caitlin's life. To dispel concerns about keeping conversation alive, she identified in advance five or six topics they might discuss. If, when together, her preplanned ideas felt forced, she would merely drop them and go with the flow of their talk. Mindful that her worth comes from Christ, not others, she wrote the following helpful self-talk to gather the courage to call Caitlin:

Situation	Helpful Self-Talk	Feelings	Behavior
Considering asking Caitlin to meet for coffee.	That Caitlin has never initiated getting together doesn't mean she wouldn't enjoy my company. I haven't reached out to many people I've been interested in getting to know. I'm not unique. A whole host of reasons have kept many people, like me, from taking action to connect.	motivated empowered	Call.
	The only way I'll find out if Caitlin wants to spend time with me is if I ask. If she doesn't, that's okay. I doubt she'd look down on me for initiating coffee, but what she thinks is out of my control and nothing to worry about. I'm not giving her or anyone else power to determine my worth—only Christ can be trusted with that. I won't let fear of rejection stop me from discovering if we might enjoy time together.	liberated self-respecting	

Situation	Helpful Self-Talk	Feelings	Behavior
	Not knowing Caitlin well gives me my first topic—I can start by asking her about her life. I want to get to know her, and most people appreciate others showing an interest in them. I don't know if she'll enjoy me; I don't know if I'll enjoy her. Different personalities appreciate different people. I won't take it personally if she doesn't show further interest, just as she need not take it personally if afterward I decide not to call again. Expanding a friendship network requires risk. No big deal. This is life for everyone. Neither of us is the judge of people's worth. Christ already established that for all of us.		

Although "dinner and a movie" probably is what people most commonly propose when initiating getting together, there are many other options also. The following list contains more suggestions for planning time with others.

TABLE **8**

Ideas for Social Activities

Hobbies	Woodworking/carving Needlework/knitting Baking/cooking Discussing novels, poetry, or nonfiction Camping/backpacking/rappelling Singing/dancing Nature walks Playing musical instruments Jigsaw puzzles Kite flying Playing a game
Sports	Walking/hiking/running Badminton/tennis/racquetball Table tennis (Ping-Pong)/pool Bicycling Football/baseball/basketball/soccer/volleyball Swimming/surfing Fishing/hunting Archery Golf Skiing/snowshoeing/ice skating Canoeing/sailing/boating Bowling Horseback riding

Miscellaneous	Attend a concert/symphony/play/opera. Go to a movie. Take courses through community education or church. Go for a drive in the country. Take in local sightseeing. Attend festivals/fairs. Visit the zoo. Go shopping. Eat at a restaurant or have a picnic. Take a cooking class. Attend a sporting event. Visit a museum or art gallery. Participate in church activities (worship services, study groups, service projects, social events). Plan a special day-trip or weekend trip. Visit the library/bookstore/coffee shop.
Volunteer Work	Churches/hospitals/schools Political party

Building a Friendship Network

Most people recognize their need for friends and work to establish meaningful connections with others. Yet sometimes, once they've secured one or two close relationships, they stop putting forth the effort to forge additional bonds. Such people risk ending up entirely alone, and the few connections they nurture entail too much pressure. No one can meet all the needs of a spouse or friend. Whether married or single, we are wise to cultivate at least five friendships with people of our own sex.

———■———

Parker was blind to his need for more friends. During the past two years, he'd spent most of his time with his girlfriend, Claire. He also enjoyed one other friend, Liam. Otherwise he saw no need to expand his social circle.

Parker and Liam played racquetball on Tuesdays and Thursdays. Life was good, Parker thought. But then, unexpectedly, within less than a month, Liam's job transferred him out of state, and Claire broke up with him. Suddenly, Parker felt abandoned, lonely, and depressed. He had no social contact, and no one offered support as he grieved the loss of Claire.

Building a social network takes effort, which was more difficult for Parker to muster when he was emotionally suffering. Yet he knew he was capable of reaching out to others. And this is true for us all, no matter how we feel. Remember—we have direct control over our behavior.

The first step is to identify potential friends. Co-workers and neighbors offer possibilities. So do interest groups, organizations, and community education classes. Parker considered joining a running club. He pondered taking a photography class, something he'd thought about for years.

Now, specifically, when he was hurting, Parker also keenly sensed the need to include in his network individuals with whom he could develop close bonds. He wanted relief from his isolation. Yet the thought of sharing his vulnerabilities soon after meeting people in a running club or photography class sounded awkward.

His mother suggested he get involved at the church he occasionally attended, maybe by volunteering to serve on a committee or help with a service project. She mentioned too that he might join a Bible study—deep conversation is often the norm at such gatherings, which was how she presented it.

Parker had never read the Bible. He imagined he would feel uncomfortable in that setting. After weighing the idea, he wrote down his self-talk to identify his fears.

Situation	Unhelpful Self-Talk	Feelings	Behavior
Considering attending a Bible study.	I'd feel strange attending *BECAUSE* I don't know much about the Bible *which is a problem because* (*WIAPB*) others there would know more than I do *WIAPB* I wouldn't fit in *BECAUSE* only biblical scholars attend Bible studies.	hesitant	Don't go.

Situation	Unhelpful Self-Talk	Feelings	Behavior
	I could be called on to state my opinion *WIAPB* I'd look stupid *BECAUSE* I don't know the Bible *WIAPB* others would look down on me *BE-CAUSE* they attend to expose and shame those who know less than they do.	intimidated	

Parker saw that his concerns were unsound. Announcements at church regularly encouraged everyone to sign up for a study. Certainly not every attendee was a scholar. His helpful self-talk convinced him to give it a chance.

Situation	Helpful Self-Talk	Feelings	Behavior
Considering attending a Bible study.	It's true that I don't know much about the Bible, but I could learn. People attend Bible studies to better understand the Bible—that's what I would have in common with them. If I'm the least knowledgeable, so be it.	motivated	Go.
	I'm not entering a competition, nor would I attend to impress anyone. I'd go to learn and meet new people. If I were called on to speak, I could give my opinion, ask a question, or pass. Questions about what I don't understand could enhance the discussion for everyone. It's unlikely anyone would attend a Bible study to expose and shame the uninformed.	determined	
	This is an opportunity for me to increase my biblical knowledge and grow in my faith. It also would be a chance for deeper conversations with others, which I don't often experience these days. Substantive discussions frequently draw people closer together. I need that right now.	optimistic	

Parker learned the hard way the value of maintaining a broad circle of friendships. A large network brings us new ideas and interests and creates opportunities for us to touch the lives of others. This provides satisfaction in living, thereby improving mental health. Having a variety of friends—one who likes to discuss books, another who talks politics or sports, someone who shares interests in music or movies, another to work out with, another who's a great confidant, and others with whom to grow in faith—enriches life.

Giving and Receiving in Social Relationships

Some people are takers. Without hesitation they ask others for anything, anytime. These frequent requests often build resentment; people feel used.

Others are givers. They constantly put themselves out for family, friends, even strangers, and refuse to let anyone help them. Accepting assistance of any kind makes them squirm. They feel vulnerable, and they also believe they would owe a debt to anyone who bestowed favors on them. Extreme takers and rigid givers both erect barriers to close relationships.

Healthy social relationships enjoy balance between giving and taking. Only taking reveals ugly self-centeredness, which obviously turns off others. At the same time, only giving is a means of staying in control and avoiding vulnerability.

We remember Jesus' gifts to us, most notably his death on the cross to reconcile us to God. Yet this same Jesus, fully God and fully man, also allowed Mary Magdalene to pour expensive perfume on his feet and minister to him in that way.[3] He requested support from his disciples as well. On the night when he was betrayed, he told Peter, James, and John, "My soul is overwhelmed with sorrow to the point of death. Stay here and keep watch with me."[4] Refusing all help, all support, places us in a superior position over those around us.

Phoebe needed to work on her willingness to receive *and* give. She and Anita had been friends for years; Anita loved art, Phoebe did not. A new art museum had opened up in town, and Phoebe knew that none of Anita's other friends had any interest in visiting. The thought that Anita might really appreciate her suggesting they go together flashed through her mind, but she instantly dismissed the idea. It turned out she needed to use the third power tool, "which is important because" (WIIB), to fully expose her faulty thinking.

Situation	Unhelpful Self-Talk	Feelings	Behavior
Consider-ing inviting Anita to visit the new art museum with me.	I don't want to spend an afternoon there *BECAUSE* art doesn't interest me *BECAUSE* I don't know much about it *which is a problem because (WIAPB)* I have no interest in learning more about it *WIAPB* I shouldn't have to put myself out that much *BECAUSE* Anita doesn't expect that from me *which is important BE-CAUSE (WIIB)* I can still have a friendship with her without torturing myself with art *WIIB* if I don't have to go the extra mile for her I won't *BECAUSE* it takes too much effort *BECAUSE* I wouldn't enjoy it *WIAPB* I should experience maximum fun every waking hour of my life.	reluctant	Don't invite.
	I don't really need to go with Anita *BECAUSE* she can go alone *BECAUSE* she doesn't need me along to enjoy the art *WIIB* if I don't have to go the extra mile for her I won't *BECAUSE* I could end up spending all my time running around accompanying friends on activities they love and I hate *BECAUSE* occasionally putting myself out for a friend would turn me into a doormat.	unmotivated	
	I don't recall Anita putting herself out a lot for me *WIIB* then I shouldn't have to for her either *BECAUSE* I don't need to work harder than her in our friendship *BECAUSE* that wouldn't be fair *WIAPB* life should be 100 percent fair.	justified	

Note how *WIIB* helped Phoebe uncover her flawed thinking. Following "Anita doesn't expect that from me" with *WIAPB* would have led her to the helpful self-talk of "I shouldn't have to do it *WIAPB* I won't learn to put myself out for others *WIAPB* I'll become more self-centered." On the other hand, *WIIB* prompts her to identify why "Anita doesn't expect that from me" is relevant to the question of whether or not to suggest a museum visit. That is, unlike *WIAPB*, *WIIB* reveals rationalizations that let Phoebe off the hook:

Situation	Unhelpful Self-Talk	Feelings	Behavior
Considering inviting Anita to visit the	Anita doesn't expect that from me *which is im-portant because (WIIB)* I can still have a friendship with her without torturing myself with art *WIIB* if	reluctant	

Situation	Unhelpful Self-Talk	Feelings	Behavior
new art museum with me.	I don't have to go the extra mile for her I won't *BECAUSE* it takes too much effort *BECAUSE* I wouldn't enjoy it *WIAPB* I should experience maximum fun every waking hour of my life.		

Phoebe's unhelpful self-talk exposed her selfish style. She understood the necessity of changing her attitude and following Christ's example of sacrificing for others. Both she and Anita would benefit.

Situation	Helpful Self-Talk	Feelings	Behavior
Considering inviting Anita to visit the new art museum with me.	I've never enjoyed art, but the afternoon wouldn't be about me. Anita and I have been friends for years. I don't know of anyone else who would go there with her, and it would be an act of love to suggest we go together. Self-sacrifice is good—it pushes me out of my self-centeredness. Who knows, I may even enjoy the afternoon and learn something. Choosing to have a curious mind about the art I encounter would certainly help.	motivated cheerful inspired	Invite Anita to go. Ask questions and engage with Anita and the art when there.
	True, Anita could go by herself, but that's not the point. Putting myself out for her would be a good thing to do. Going wouldn't mean I'd have to devote my future to accompanying friends on activities they love and I hate. Setting aside my interests for the sake of my friends sometimes would not turn me into a doormat. It would be following Christ's example of how to treat others.		
	Cut the "it's not fair" thinking! I'm not keeping score of who puts themselves out most. It would mean a lot to Anita if I happily accompanied her, and so I will.		

Serving Others

When she visited the art gallery, Phoebe set aside her interests for the sake of someone else. This is what Christ instructs his followers to do. Give without looking to receive, and amazingly, much comes back. That was Phoebe's experience again, several months later, when she anticipated being alone on Thanksgiving with nowhere to go. Rather than sit home and bemoan her plight, she volunteered to serve dinner at a homeless shelter. Choosing to focus on helping others transformed her potentially lonely and miserable holiday into one of her most meaningful and memorable ever.

Countless needs exist, including packaging food at Feed My Starving Children, delivering food through Meals on Wheels, volunteering at schools, churches, or hospitals, and mission work in North America or overseas.

The apostle Paul wrote to the Corinthian church,

> Since you excel in everything—in faith, in speech, in knowledge, in complete earnestness and in the love we have kindled in you—see that you also excel in this grace of giving.[5]

Paradoxically, through giving to others we receive and fortify our mental health.

TAKING
CHARGE
of YOUR
EMOTIONS

8

Defeating Depression

The LORD is close to the brokenhearted
and saves those who are crushed in spirit.[1]

Part IV integrates all the relationships explored in parts I, II,
and III as a prescription for emotional health. This section,
which includes chapters on depression, anxiety, and anger, shows
how to use these relationships—between thoughts, feelings, and
behaviors; with Christ; and with people—to overcome painful
emotions. They all offer specific resources for finding relief, and
the book closes with a look at how these relationships offer joy.

Our focus turns now to depression as we examine various
intensities of this emotional challenge. Let's start by meeting
Rochelle, who struggled with the Sunday evening blues.

Around four p.m. each Sunday, the fog of melancholy started
rolling in. Rochelle dreaded this unwelcome visitor, a vague, diffuse gloom that pierced her awareness, but she considered the
rendezvous unavoidable. She saw no point in writing self-talk.

Nothing bad had happened. No terrible "situation" confronted her.

Perhaps biochemistry was the culprit. Yet if her thinking really produced her feelings, maybe some thoughts buried deep in her mind were generating this anxious sadness. Tired of the darkness, and admitting she had nothing to lose, Rochelle sat down one Sunday evening to use the Seven Steps to identify her self-talk. Selecting specific words from the Feelings List (see chapter 2) that described her emotional state provided clues to help uncover her thoughts.

Situation	Unhelpful Self-Talk	Feelings	Behavior
It's Sunday evening, and I feel depressed.	The weekend I so looked forward to is over *which is a problem because* (*WIAPB*) once again I'm let down *BECAUSE* I didn't accomplish half of what I wanted to do and didn't have time to relax *WIAPB* tomorrow I return to the grind of work *WIAPB* I have no free time during the week *WIAPB* my life is a treadmill *BECAUSE* I never have fun *BECAUSE* all I do is work.	disappointed	Passive. Fret away the evening. Don't call anyone.
	It's Sunday evening and I'm alone *WIAPB* I wish I could be with someone *BECAUSE* I feel isolated and restless *WIAPB* no one's available to join me *BECAUSE* I didn't arrange to get together with anyone *WIAPB* I can't call someone now *BECAUSE* they probably have plans already *WIAPB* people might decline my invite *WIAPB* I couldn't handle a no *BECAUSE* that would mean they don't like me *BECAUSE* people always drop whatever they're doing if someone they care about asks to get together.	lonely	
	I go back to work tomorrow *WIAPB* I hate my job *BECAUSE* my boss is so demanding *BECAUSE* she has unrealistic expectations on what I can accomplish *WIAPB* I'm under constant stress *BECAUSE* I can't talk to her *BECAUSE* she's stressed too and has no one available to ease my load *BECAUSE* the company has a hiring freeze *WIAPB* I have no choice but to live with stress all day.	full of dread	

By labeling her precise feelings and then discovering the self-talk behind each one, Rochelle realized her Sunday evening blues were not inevitable after all. Her specific interpretation of Sunday night created her malaise. She had unknowingly slipped into the habit of viewing it through a negative filter. At last aware of the problem, she could turn around her thinking.

Rochelle's unhelpful self-talk identified several issues that needed to be addressed. The power tool of *problem-solving* (see chapter 2 to review power tools for helpful self-talk) would assist her in better planning and organizing her weekend. Her unhelpful self-talk made clear her need to arrange in advance for companionship whenever possible on Sunday nights. She also realized the importance of monitoring the self-talk that contributed to her experience of stress at work. The *reframing* power tool would help her find relief as well. She could choose gratitude instead of focusing on complaints about her job.

Situation	Helpful Self-Talk	Feelings	Behavior
It's Sunday evening, and I feel depressed.	I'll likely be more satisfied with my weekend if I plan it better. I know I feel deprived when Sunday evening arrives and I didn't take time to relax. Now, whenever possible, I can set aside at least a couple weekend hours for free time. I can also be careful to set reasonable goals about what I might accomplish. Despite my sense of deprivation right now, it's not true that all I do is work or have no fun-time during the week. I played golf last weekend and met a friend for dinner Tuesday night.	determined	Set realistic goals for the weekend. Set aside time to relax. Make Sunday evening plans in advance.
	I'm typically lonely when I have no plans on Sunday night. Enough of this passivity! I will be proactive and plan ahead, arranging when possible to get together with friends or family. I could volunteer somewhere, attend a church service, or find another activity that gets me out of the house too. I have nothing to lose calling someone even tonight. I won't take it personally if people decline; spontaneity works sometimes. If no one's available I'll do a "solitary activity." With or without companionship, I will make this a good evening.	in control	Call someone tonight. If no one is free, select from the Solitary Activities list.
	I'll focus on what's good about my job and be grateful I'm employed. Yes, my boss is demanding,	encouraged	

Situation	Helpful Self-Talk	Feelings	Behavior
	but she works just as hard. Work is interesting and rewarding—just stressful. I must work efficiently but need not choose stress-producing self-talk. I'll start monitoring and changing my self-talk tomorrow to minimize stress.		

You can find the Solitary Activities list to which Rochelle referred in chapter 6. Writing the helpful self-talk corrected her thinking and pointed her to behaviors that could help change her mood as well.

Rochelle was challenged by occasional melancholy. Other people suffer from grief or more intense depression. I do not here address formal diagnoses, such as Major Depression, but rather the full spectrum of depressive mood—from fleeting sadness to severe depression that is brief or lengthy in duration. The ideas in this chapter can be applied to combat any degree of this emotion because the thoughts and behaviors that create depression share certain characteristics, no matter how mild or intense or long-lasting the emotional pain. Those characteristic approaches to life will be explored in the pages to follow and also will serve to define *depression* for purposes of this chapter.

Accepting Sadness and Grief

It is important to note that we need not instantly take charge of our self-talk and behavior every time we notice emotional pain. Sometimes we prefer and choose to just sit with sadness for a while. That's all right. At other times in life we face losses like death, or divorce, or geographical relocation that we must grieve. I hold back from immediately teaching the Seven Steps to people who have recently experienced such distress. Standard journaling better helps the newly bereaved. As long as they are neither suicidal nor homicidal, they can use "stream-of-consciousness" recording to describe their sorrow and anguish, without trying to control those feelings in any way, to help purge the pain.

No one can cite an optimal length of time for expressing unchallenged grief. Each person and situation is unique, but at some point grievers benefit from beginning to examine how they are interpreting life around them. And starting occasionally to use the Seven Steps does not mean they can never again allow themselves times of uncontested sadness.

Gradually, however, the bereaved may more frequently identify and turn around thinking that corresponds to pain. Events that trigger stabs of sorrow may sometimes catch survivors of loss off guard for the rest of their lives, despite these efforts. Yet as time passes they can begin to compartmentalize their sadness, choosing helpful interpretations of life increasingly often while still allowing moments to mourn.

Fundamentals of Brain Care for Emotional Health

Before examining in depth how to defeat depression, let's briefly consider the health of our brains, the physical source of our emotions. Proper thyroid levels are vital to healthy brain activity, and, as we've discussed, new learning helps keep brains strong. Other actions play key roles in supporting brain fitness as well. Fueling ourselves with a nutritious diet, eating a balanced breakfast, minimizing sugar, and drinking plenty of water all affect brain function. Exercise oxygenates the brain and releases endorphins, which are natural mood enhancers. Plenty of sleep also helps the brain perform its best. Optimal emotional health requires that we provide our bodies and our brains, in particular, with what they need to operate effectively.

With its basic physical needs addressed, we can examine how the thoughts this organ produces can create depression.

Characteristics of Depressive Thinking

The frequency, intensity, and duration of depressive moods directly correlate to our self-talk and behavior. Key to finding relief from any emotion on the depressive continuum is changing the thoughts and actions that produce the pain. Familiarity with the "cognitive triad of depression" and the "locus of control" theory can help us recognize ways of thinking that contribute to depression.

The Cognitive Triad of Depression

Depressed people develop habits of interpreting life in a negative, pessimistic way. As we reviewed in chapter 1, Dr. Aaron Beck identified the "cognitive triad of depression,"[2] three beliefs depressed people tend to hold: they view themselves, life around them, and the future through a negative lens. Without consciously choosing this filter, depressed people see life through shades of gray.

Jill's thinking reflected the "cognitive triad of depression" ever since her boyfriend, Aiden, broke up with her last month. Her pain was intense. With his departure, her life suddenly looked entirely dreary. Now either deep pain or alarming numbness overshadowed every waking moment. Jill questioned herself and could not imagine ever again finding life pleasant and enjoyable.

Situation	Unhelpful Self-Talk	Feelings	Behavior
My boyfriend of two years broke up with me last month.	Aiden broke up with me *BECAUSE* he isn't sure he loves me *BECAUSE* after two years of dating he still doesn't know if he wants to spend his life with me *which is a problem because (WIAPB)* I can't imagine my life without him *BECAUSE* he's my best friend, constant companion, and has brought so much joy to my life *WIAPB* everything reminds me of him *WIAPB* I'll never get over him *BECAUSE* people can never recover from losing a love.	devastated	Passive.

Situation	Unhelpful Self-Talk	Feelings	Behavior
	This pain is now my only connection to Aiden *which is important BECAUSE* (*WIIB*) my suffering is a continuous reminder of him *WIIB* I won't let go of the pain *BECAUSE* I want him to be prominent in my life always *BECAUSE* I can't imagine a good life without him *BECAUSE* he alone holds the key to my happiness.	desperate	
	I'm not good enough for Aiden *BECAUSE* he doesn't love me *WIAPB* there must be something wrong with me *BECAUSE* otherwise he wouldn't have broken up with me *BECAUSE* he's the ultimate judge of my worth.	rejected	Cry.
	No one else cares about me like Aiden did *BECAUSE* I was the most important person in his life *WIAPB* now I don't play that role with anyone *WIAPB* I need to be someone's top priority *BECAUSE* my security is based on being Number One in someone else's life.	insecure	Mope.
	I miss Aiden so much *WIAPB* he was my favorite companion *WIAPB* no one else fills that void *BECAUSE* other people don't bring me the joy he brought me *WIAPB* I don't feel like reaching out to family or friends *BECAUSE* I don't enjoy them like I did Aiden *WIAPB* it doesn't make sense for me to spend time with others unless they meet my every need.	lonely	Withdraw from others.

Jill needs to recognize the cognitive triad of depression in her current insecurity, dissatisfaction with life, and conviction that this intense suffering will never end. These beliefs create depression.

After a significant loss, people commonly find it difficult to believe they will ever again enjoy life. Painful emotions currently dominate Jill—they are the engine of her train (see chapter 3). While she must allow herself to grieve the end of her relationship with Aiden, she can also keep some perspective, even in her suffering. Then, as time passes, she can more and more take charge of her thinking and behaviors to find emotional relief.

The cognitive triad of depression need not find safe harbor in her mind forever. Eventually she can return emotions to the caboose of her train.

Situation	Helpful Self-Talk	Feelings	Behavior
My boy-friend of two years broke up with me last month.	I love Aiden and am crushed that he doesn't see a future with me. I do need to grieve this breakup. It's natural for pain to accompany reminders of him—this happens constantly right now because we did so much together. As time passes and I experience more of life without him, those connections will weaken, and the pain will diminish. Most people have suffered a broken heart at least once, yet they go on to have satisfying lives.	encouraged	Read the Bible and pray—focus on Christ.
	I'm giving Aiden too much power when I say I can't have a good life without him. The First Commandment is "I am the Lord your God. You shall have no other gods before me." I'm making Aiden my god when I say he holds the key to my happiness. Only God can be trusted with this power over my life. God has a plan for me; I've been seeking that plan. This breakup doesn't limit his ability to guide me down a fulfilling, satisfying path, even though just yet I can't imagine a good life without him. Few can envision future happiness right after someone they love goes away. Believing the sadness will always last is a symptom of depression. I have to grieve this loss, but I'm stubbornly wasting time and energy by purposely holding on to emotional pain to stay connected. My hope is in Christ. I choose to let go of Aiden and trust God with my life.	determined	Arrange to get together with friends and family.
	No one is perfect. I can take this opportunity to examine and correct any contribution I made to problems in our relationship. But only Christ is the ultimate judge of my worth. He created me, loves me, and says I'm worthwhile. I have unshakable esteem through Christ.	self-respecting	
	It feels wonderful to be the most important person in someone's life, but placing my security in human hands makes me too vulnerable. Christ, the only solid source of security, will never abandon me.	confident	
	Right now my first choice for companionship is Aiden, but he has exited my life. I do enjoy other friends and family. I can call and make plans to spend time with them. I can also escape some of my sadness by serving others. I refuse to sit and mope. Aiden did not take all that is good with him. I will stay engaged with life and focus on my purpose through Christ. Gradually I'll feel better.	motivated	Look for opportunities to serve others.

The *"Locus of Control"* Theory

Jill can choose to prevent this painful breakup from dominating her life indefinitely. Her helpful self-talk reveals thoughts and actions she may take to feel better. Capitalizing on what is inside her control to improve her life would reflect an "internal locus of control."

Psychologist Julian Rotter developed the "locus of control" theory, suggesting that each person falls somewhere on a continuum between the extreme poles of an entirely internal or entirely external locus of control. Individuals tending toward an internal locus identify and act on the power they have in the situations they encounter. Those with a more external locus believe that circumstances or other people determine what happens to them.

Some of the first words attributed to humans reveal an external-locus-of-control mind-set. When confronting Adam and Eve in the garden of Eden, God asked Adam,

> "Have you eaten from the tree that I commanded you not to eat from?" The man said, "The woman you put here with me—she gave me some fruit from the tree, and I ate it." Then the LORD God said to the woman, "What is this you have done?" The woman said, "The serpent deceived me, and I ate."[3]

Both Adam and Eve portrayed themselves as helpless victims. Adam first blamed God, then Eve, for his choice. Next Eve blamed the serpent. When we fail to recognize and/or act on what we can do to improve life, we miss out on the good that is available to us and often suffer unnecessarily.

It's easy for us to fall into the trap of considering ourselves at the mercy of our situation. This frame of mind, however, can contribute to depression. Take Roger, for example. He regularly viewed life through a negative and pessimistic lens and also routinely saw himself as powerless to improve his life in any way. His response to the news that he was currently earning an F in biology reflected his external locus of control.

Situation	Unhelpful Self-Talk	Feelings	Behavior
I just learned my mid-semester grade in biology is an F.	Mr. Nelson is a terrible teacher BECAUSE he says I have an F in his class BECAUSE he can't teach biology BECAUSE others have gotten bad grades too, and they think he's a rotten teacher which is a problem because (WIAPB) I'm stuck with a lousy teacher WIAPB there's no way I can learn the material BECAUSE Mr. Nelson can't teach.	victimized	Passive.
	I hate biology BECAUSE it's so boring BECAUSE it isn't relevant to my life BECAUSE I know I never want to do anything related to science WIAPB I have to put up with this awful class BECAUSE it's a requirement for graduation WIAPB I can't pass the class BECAUSE Mr. Nelson can't teach.	unmotivated	Blame Mr. Nelson.
	I have to take the F BECAUSE I've studied and tried, but can't pass the tests BECAUSE I have a bad teacher WIAPB there's nothing I can do to pass the class BECAUSE it's already halfway through the semester WIAPB it's too late to turn things around BECAUSE I got F's on two tests WIAPB I can't pass the class.	defeated	Take the F.

Roger considered himself powerless in the face of this and virtually every other challenge he faced. Now a "bad teacher" was sealing his fate. Quickly giving up, he unnecessarily embraced defeat once again. Yet this response to his mid-semester grade was not the only option. Bad teachers certainly exist, but Mr. Nelson was not one of them. Looking around would reveal to Roger that most other students successfully learn biology in Mr. Nelson's class. He could adopt an internal locus of control.

Situation	Helpful Self-Talk	Feelings	Behavior
I just learned my mid-semester grade in biology is an F.	Most people aren't flunking Mr. Nelson's class and only a few of us complain about him, so maybe the problem is mostly with me. I'll make an appointment with him to go over my last test, see what I missed,	motivated empowered self-respecting	Make an appointment with Mr. Nelson to get extra help.

Situation	Helpful Self-Talk	Feelings	Behavior
	and ask for strategies to help prepare for the next one. If after meeting with him and studying hard I still don't grasp the material, I'll ask for help from students who are succeeding or look for a tutor. I refuse to accept that I can't learn biology.		If Mr. Nelson can't adequately explain the concepts to me, ask for help from students who do understand or hire a tutor.
	I create my feelings with my self-talk and behavior. I hate biology because I tell myself it's miserable and irrelevant. I passively endure each class, put no energy into homework, then fall behind again. I can think and behave differently. I don't know my future or whether the material from this class may someday be important to me. I can choose to have a curious mind and tell myself I'm privileged to learn. I'll pay attention in class, ask questions when I don't understand, and keep up with my homework.		Pay attention in class and ask questions when I don't understand.
	It's a cop-out to blame Mr. Nelson and take the F. There's still half a semester to go before final grades. This is a wake-up call. I choose to get in gear today and learn biology.		Keep up with the homework and ask questions about anything I don't understand.

By identifying and acting on what's in his control, Roger can better learn biology and improve his grade. He can also improve his mental health.

Naomi, a retired nurse, could apply the same strategy to dealing with winter in Minnesota. Naomi despises winter and fully expects to feel depressed throughout the season, an expectation realized every year. Living in this northern state, she miserably endures a significant portion of her days, and her external locus of control governs her approach to life.

Situation	Unhelpful Self-Talk	Feelings	Behavior
It's January.	I hate winter *BECAUSE* it's freezing cold outside *which is a problem because* (*WIAPB*) doing	depressed	Passive.

141

Situation	Unhelpful Self-Talk	Feelings	Behavior
	anything takes so much effort *BECAUSE* I have to put on coat, hat, scarf, gloves, and boots just to step out of my house *WIAPB* it's a hassle and I'm so bound up I can hardly move *WIAPB* I'm still miserable when I'm outside *BECAUSE* the wind is bone-chilling *WIAPB* I'm essentially housebound for five months *WIAPB* I go stir-crazy inside *BECAUSE* there's nothing to do *BECAUSE* no indoor projects or activities interest me.		Sleep (hibernate).
	It's so dark and dreary in the winter *BECAUSE* the days are short and ugly, and dirty snow covers the ground *WIAPB* I just have to endure it *BECAUSE* it's the worst time of the year *BECAUSE* it's cold and miserable *WIAPB* there's no way I can enjoy this season.	unmotivated	

Naomi indulged herself in helpless self-pity throughout the winter months. She recognized no other choice. Winter in Minnesota was treacherous at worst, dismal at best. Yet whenever she chose, she possessed the power to discard her external locus of control. With helpful self-talk she could cultivate an internal locus instead.

Situation	Helpful Self-Talk	Feelings	Behavior
It's January.	I refuse to let my environment determine my happiness. Enough of this passive malaise each winter! I have choices regarding my thoughts about and behaviors during colder times of the year. Variety makes life more interesting. Each season offers something good. Winter is a great time to tackle my many indoor projects. Plus, I don't need to isolate myself at home. I have plenty of clothes to keep me warm when I venture out, and the brisk air can be invigorating. It's worth the effort to get together with others. Endless opportunities to serve could provide meaning and purpose during these months as well.	empowered determined energized	Do indoor projects. Volunteer. Invite people over and make plans to go out with others. Review lists of Solitary Activities, Social Activities, Learning Opportunities. Plan cozy nights at home.

Recall that the lists Naomi references were presented earlier (Learning Opportunities and Solitary Activities, chapter 6; Social Activities, chapter 7).

Like Naomi, before she used the Seven Steps, over time we may fail to recognize and capitalize on what is within our control to improve life. Such neglect fosters depression. Although we clearly cannot control all that happens to us, we are wise to check the belief that our environment determines our destiny. We enrich life around us when we identify what is inside our control and act on positive options, the next consideration of this chapter.

Characteristic Depressive Behaviors

Certain behaviors accompany depression, such as passivity and withdrawal, and, as with our self-talk, we can directly control our behaviors. Therefore, it makes sense to monitor and make adaptive choices with both. If we perceive a pattern of isolation or inactivity developing, we can stop and correct the slide. Regardless of our feelings we can choose to act and to end idle seclusion.

For instance, consider Marissa. She was depressed. She struggled to undertake even the smallest task. Mustering the energy to walk into her kitchen, open the cupboard, take out a pan, and put it on the stove seemed daunting. Reclining on her couch whenever possible, she saw no light at the end of this tunnel.

She had sought professional help but found no relief. She balked at her friend's suggestion to use the Steps as a means of taking charge of her thoughts and behavior. Initially the idea sounded insensitive and ignorant, revealing the friend's failure to comprehend the depths of her depression. How could she write out anything when in such a dismal place?

Yet Marissa wanted release from her depression. Finally, one day she picked up the note pad and pen on the table next to her. She jotted down the unhelpful self-talk associated with each of her feelings.

Situation	Unhelpful Self-Talk	Feelings	Behavior
Sitting at home, aware of feeling depressed.	I hate this depression BECAUSE it robs me of joy in living BECAUSE I constantly feel sad and empty BECAUSE my life is meaningless BECAUSE no one needs me or cares about me BECAUSE I don't make a difference BECAUSE there's nothing special about me BECAUSE I have no talents that really stand out which is a problem BECAUSE (WIAPB) anyone worthwhile has at least one talent no one else possesses.	hopeless	Passive.
	I feel like a robot just going through the motions WIAPB I'm numb WIAPB I used to garden, get together with friends, and watch football, but now I don't care about anything WIAPB I must care BECAUSE I can't make myself do anything until I care BECAUSE I have to feel motivated before I can take action BECAUSE I'm incapable of moving my body.	unmotivated	Sit around and do nothing.
	There's nothing I can do to get relief from this depression BECAUSE it's like a dark cloud that just descends on me WIAPB I'm stuck with this sadness BECAUSE my feelings are completely out of my control.	powerless	
	I wish I could be happy like everyone else BECAUSE I shouldn't have to suffer like this BECAUSE life should be easier BECAUSE pain has no value BECAUSE it just torments me BECAUSE it leaves me barely able to get through each day, much less capable of putting out for others BECAUSE I can't get together with others and visit with them BECAUSE I'm unable to move my body or speak.	bitter	

No wonder she was depressed. Who wouldn't feel despondent with such thoughts dominating her mind? Marissa's unhelpful self-talk exposed the cognitive triad of depression: a negative view of herself ("no one needs me," "I don't make a difference"), a negative view of life around her ("I feel like a robot just going through the motions," "I don't care about anything"), and a negative view of the future ("There's nothing I can do to get relief").

Placing a lot of stock in her faulty beliefs, she continually fed her downcast mood. She also waited to feel better before considering taking action to engage with life. Feelings were in her train's engine. Marissa forgot she directly controls her behavior and that no matter how she felt she could move her body and get in gear. Feelings belong in the caboose.

Helpful self-talk challenged her previous paralyzing assumptions.

Situation	Helpful Self-Talk	Feelings	Behavior
Sitting at home, aware of feeling depressed.	It's ridiculous to say an exceptional talent is necessary to be a person of value. My worth is not based on how I compare to others. Thank God for that, because no one stays at the top of any heap for long! Christ created me for a purpose and established my worth. My purpose through him can't be taken away no matter how I feel. I can serve others regardless of my mood. Satisfaction comes from focusing on others, and that can help fill my emptiness.	blessed	Write self-talk daily for at least a month. Garden. Watch football. Get together with friends. Read the Bible daily. Get involved at church. Focus on my purpose—serve others.
	Not finding pleasure in daily life is just a symptom of depression, like a runny nose is a symptom of a cold. When the depression is gone I'll feel happiness again. Emotional disconnectedness from what I used to thoroughly enjoy feels strange, but this numbness will pass after I take charge of my self-talk and behaviors for a while. Whether I feel like it or not, I'll work in the garden, watch football, and initiate getting together with friends. I'll also go back to church. Feelings play too prominent a role in my life—I'm giving them too much respect.	self-respecting	
	I'm not at the mercy of my emotions. Thoughts and actions create feelings, and I can take charge of both. I'm interpreting life in a pessimistic way these days. I can write self-talk daily for at least a month to recognize these negative attitudes and train my mind to think in a more helpful way.	determined	
	Even though I feel made of cement, I'm very capable of moving my body and speaking. I need to kick feelings off center stage. Feelings are fickle and don't deserve such power. I will lead with helpful self-talk and helpful behavior. More desirable feelings will eventually follow.	motivated	

Situation	Helpful Self-Talk		Feelings	Behavior
	It's not true that everyone else feels happy. All people suffer sometimes; I can choose how I respond to pain. I could decide to learn from this and become a more empathic person. I can also develop more emotional muscle when I use skills to take charge of my thoughts and behaviors. Additionally, suffering heightens my awareness of my reliance on God. I don't need to seek out or purposely prolong pain, but I can ask God to bring good from my suffering. A life free from affliction wouldn't help my relationships. People who have responded to pain in a healthy way are easier to talk to and seemingly have more depth and compassion. Suffering doesn't make me bad company—I do that myself. Being distressed doesn't mean I have to concentrate mostly on myself when with others. It requires effort, but I can purposely act to get involved with others and focus more on them.			

Once more, recall the trains introduced in chapter 3. Trains powered by feelings are destined for trouble. Waiting to feel better before taking action, like writing the Seven Steps daily, working out at the gym, engaging with and serving other people, and getting involved at church, may yield a life of passivity and emptiness. Behaviors need to lead feelings; feelings belong in the caboose.

Employing Relationships to Defeat Depression

Take Charge of Your Emotions has presented three types of relationships that help us find relief from emotional pain: (1) between thoughts, feelings, and behaviors; (2) with Jesus Christ; and (3) with people. Let's reflect further now on how each assists in overcoming depression.

The Relationship Between Thoughts, Feelings, and Behaviors

Feelings and behaviors can serve as valuable signals, alerting us that depression is knocking at our door. If feelings of

146

unhappiness or discontentment intrude and appear ready to settle in, or passivity and isolation become regular behaviors, use the Seven Steps to identify your specific feelings and the self-talk that created each of them. Note what behaviors follow, and then turn around unhelpful thoughts and actions. Take charge of your thoughts and behaviors, remembering that you can directly control them both. (It may be helpful to review chapter 2, which explains these Steps. Read appendix B as well, which provides additional information on how to use the Steps most effectively and shows how to solve issues you may encounter when implementing this tool.)

Once again, I recommend that people who frequently suffer depressed moods write out the Steps once a day for an extended period, with the goal of automatically interpreting life in a helpful way about 90 percent of the time. Usually, this requires about four weeks of almost daily writing, depending on the severity of the depression. Especially when beginning this process, people usually cannot finish all the steps in half an hour, but each day the writing from the previous day's thirty-minute session can be continued. After finishing one Steps exercise, begin another until the thirty minutes have passed.

As the weeks go by, some people run out of ideas of what to address in the Steps. Any cause of emotional discomfort can serve as the Situation, no matter if it's a core problem or minor distress, or whether it involves the past, present, or future. The same problems can be addressed repeatedly too, as long as previous writing is not merely copied—that does not adequately exercise the brain. It can also be useful to keep a running list of problems to write about as they come to mind throughout the day. Then consult this list when the half-hour writing time arrives.

Remember, writing the Seven Steps daily for at least a month requires about the same time and effort that people regularly devote to physical workouts. As with physical exercise, many find this process discouraging at first. It takes a while to become adept at writing the Steps, and at first the helpful self-talk only remains in the mind a few minutes before the unhelpful once again intrudes. As the days and weeks pass, however, helpful self-talk becomes more prominent in our thinking and eventually becomes more and more automatic.

Through this process, endeavor to develop an attitude of gratitude in all circumstances, as the apostle Paul advised. Additionally, cultivate an internal locus of control, diligently working to identify what is inside your control to improve your mental health. Then act on your opportunities.

A Relationship With Jesus Christ

Focusing on a relationship with Christ can also help relieve depression. Jesus frees us of the burden of our sins, and because of this forgiveness we need not suffer perpetual guilt due to our failings. He also supplies hope in all circumstances, no matter how bleak they may appear. He offers us comfort and strength by his constant presence on earth, and Christians await a bright future in heaven.

Choosing him as our Guide through life provides us unshakable worth and purpose as well. Worth through Christ allows us to risk failure and live life abundantly and vigorously. Purpose each day with him protects us from despair, no matter what we encounter.

Knowing *how* to follow Christ—knowledge of his teachings—enables us to more fully reap the mental health benefits of a relationship with him. Attending church, Sunday school classes, Bible reading, Bible studies, and prayer help us discover the truth and understand God's ways. We will never fully comprehend his mind. Neither can we with certainty declare his will every time we must make a decision. Yet his Spirit and biblical wisdom inform our decisions, alerting us to steer clear of pitfalls and directing us down paths of fulfillment.

Those who've never read the Bible or who have difficulties motivating themselves to consistently read Scripture might consider purchasing the *NIV Student Bible*.[4] The notes by Philip Yancey and Tim Stafford printed throughout help people comfortably read this book that may have previously intimidated or bored them. If you read Scripture, you might start a notebook of verses that would speak to and strengthen you when confronted with problems. The following passages, referenced in my notebook, have comforted me in times of sadness:

> Why, my soul, are you downcast?
>> Why so disturbed within me?
> Put your hope in God,
>> for I will yet praise him,
>> my Savior and my God.[5]

> There is surely a future hope for you,
>> and your hope will not be cut off.[6]

"I know the plans I have for you," declares the LORD, "plans to prosper you and not to harm you, plans to give you hope and a future."[7]

Do not let your hearts be troubled. You believe in God; believe also in me [Jesus].[8]

I [Jesus] have told you these things, so that in me you may have peace. In this world you will have trouble. But take heart! I have overcome the world.[9]

Who shall separate us from the love of Christ? Shall trouble or hardship or persecution or famine or nakedness or danger or sword? . . . No, in all these things we are more than conquerors through him who loved us. For I [Paul] am convinced that neither death nor life, neither angels nor demons, neither the present nor the future, nor any powers, neither height nor depth, nor anything else in all creation, will be able to separate us from the love of God that is in Christ Jesus our Lord.[10]

One thing I [Paul] do: Forgetting what is behind and straining toward what is ahead, I press on toward the goal to win the prize for which God has called me heavenward in Christ Jesus.[11]

Rejoice always, pray continually, give thanks in all circumstances; for this is God's will for you in Christ Jesus.[12]

Relationships With People

Human relationships play a vital role in combating depression as well. We can help ward off despair by developing loving relationships with ourselves and others using strategies presented in chapters 6 and 7. If emotional pain regularly confronts you at certain times of the week, such as weekend evenings or Sunday afternoons, make plans in advance for those hours. See the lists of Learning Opportunities (chapter 6), Solitary Activities (chapter 6), and Social Activities (chapter 7) for ideas of what you might enjoy alone or with others. Whether single or married, act on what is within your control to optimize life for yourself and those around you. Engage in service to others, following Christ's instructions. Losing ourselves to help others relieves depression, replacing melancholy with glimmers of satisfaction and fulfillment.

9

Overcoming Anxiety

Cast all your anxiety on him because he cares for you.[1]

The math test had just begun, but already panic had set in. Evan had no clue how to solve the first problem, despite studying for hours the night before. Now the second question confused him too. Catastrophic thoughts flooded his mind as he struggled to focus on the paper before him.

This was not a new experience for Evan. In fact, he had developed a pattern of quickly predicting doom whenever he could not immediately and confidently respond to exam questions.

While certainly he should not spend important testing minutes writing self-talk, later that evening Evan could revisit that agonizing hour to figure out why he froze up again on a test. Identifying the thinking that created his anxiety could prepare him to recognize similar troublesome interpretations of exams in the future. Writing the helpful self-talk would then equip him to counter alarming thoughts during his next math test.

Here is what he discovered:

Situation	Unhelpful Self-Talk	Feelings	Behavior
I'm begin- ning my math test, and I don't know how to solve the first two problems.	I don't know these answers *which is a problem because* (*WIAPB*) I likely won't know the oth- ers either *BECAUSE* I can't think *WIAPB* I'll fail the test *WIAPB* I'll fail the class *WIAPB* I'll never graduate *WIAPB* I'll never get a good job *WIAPB* my life will be ruined.	frantic	Sit and stew. Can't concentrate.
	I don't know what to do *BECAUSE* I can't an- swer these *WIAPB* time is passing *WIAPB* soon the teacher will collect our papers *WIAPB* I can't solve the problems *WIAPB* I'll fail the test.	overwhelmed	

Threats of danger plagued Evan's self-talk during his test. Struggling to answer the first two questions, he focused on his inability to think and the teacher's upcoming call for the exams. He also quickly predicted he would fail not only the test but also the class, the F's carrying ominous long-term implications. These dangers seemed quite reasonable when floating unchal- lenged in his mind. They terrified him.

By focusing on these threats, Evan wasted valuable moments during the hour. His scary self-talk scrambled his thinking, mak- ing it nearly impossible to concentrate well on math. That evening when writing out the Seven Steps, he identified another interpre- tation of his situation that was just as believable as the fearful talk. This helpful self-talk could compose him at his next exam.

Situation	Helpful Self-Talk	Feelings	Behavior
I'm begin- ning my math test, and I don't know how to solve the first two problems.	It's not uncommon to need a little time to get comfortable and warm up to a test. I'll just keep reading through the exam till I find a problem that looks easier. I studied and did fine on the homework. I'm not remembering right now how to solve the problem because I'm tel- ling myself scary, awful things, making it hard to think. This is only one test. After I look through it a little longer I'll likely recall how to do some of these problems. Even if I don't, it isn't the end of the world. I'm not going to flunk the	more confident more relaxed more in control	Read through the test and start with the easiest problems. Concen- trate on the test.

Situation	Helpful Self-Talk	Feelings	Behavior
	class from doing poorly on this test; even if I do flunk, it won't mean I can't graduate. It's absurd to say that failing one test could ruin my life! What's in my control now is to use my time to read through the exam and try my best. I can do that. The outcome I leave with Christ.		

Test anxiety was not Evan's only emotional challenge. His habitual interpretations of life in general also frequently produced fear. The ideas presented in this chapter can be applied to combat anxious challenges ranging from occasional worry to near constant and long-lasting extreme anxiety. The characteristic thoughts and behaviors that create anxiety, whether mild or intense, rare or frequent, new or long-standing, will be explored in the pages to follow. They will also serve to define *anxiety* for purposes of this chapter.[2]

Characteristics of Anxious Thinking

Dr. Aaron Beck observed that the self-talk of anxious people revolves around "themes of danger,"[3] as was noted in chapter 1. Predictions of suffering harm, beyond one's ability to manage, feed the sense of danger. Anxious thinking is often focused on the future; upcoming change is interpreted as particularly threatening. Although fear may be linked to very specific concerns, anxiety thrives on general scary statements.

Maximizing Harm, Minimizing Coping Capabilities

Evan reframed his challenge when stumped on his math test and hence diminished his perception of danger. He made no declaration that he would ace the exam; rather, he used the Seven Steps to realistically consider his situation and rein in wildly frightening thoughts. The anxious impulse runs counter to this practice. According to Dr. Beck, anxious people "maximize the likelihood of harm and minimize their ability to cope."[4] Scary thoughts freely harass those prone to anxiety, predicting terrible outcomes that will undo vulnerable victims.

Roberta's thinking illustrates this style. All week she anticipated presenting her marketing plan at work—her first time speaking before management. Multiple fears tormented her when she imagined the boardroom debut. Ruminating on this destroyed her appetite and disturbed her sleep.

The night before her talk, worn ragged by the stress and desperate for relief, Roberta decided to use the Seven Steps. She understood her anxiety once her unhelpful thinking was exposed.

Situation	Unhelpful Self-Talk	Feelings	Behavior
Tomorrow I present my marketing proposal to management.	Many higher-ups are going to hear my proposal *which is a problem because* (*WIAPB*) someone might ask a question I can't answer *WIAPB* I'll look incompetent *BECAUSE* I'm expected to know my stuff *WIAPB* I'll be passed over for advancement and could even lose my job *BECAUSE* those in power will no longer respect me *BECAUSE* knowledgeable people are never stumped.	intimidated	Don't sleep again tonight.
	I won't be able to think clearly *BECAUSE* I'll be so nervous *WIAPB* I'll lose my train of thought and stand there babbling with a blank look *WIAPB* I won't be able to recover from blunders *WIAPB* my superiors will be dismayed *WIAPB* my future here will be ruined *WIAPB* no other company will ever hire me *BECAUSE* this presentation will mark the end of my career.	pressured	Try to bluff it if I don't know the answer to a question.
	My hands will shake, my voice may tremble *BECAUSE* these things happen whenever I speak before a group *WIAPB* those in power won't respect me *BECAUSE* they'll focus on my anxious look *BECAUSE* they're more interested in how I control my nerves than in my proposal's content.	panicky	Focus on shaking hands and trembling voice rather than reaching my audience.

When envisioning her presentation, Roberta maximized the likelihood of harm. She imagined irreparably damaging her working reputation, losing not only her job but even all hope for future employment. She also minimized her ability to cope, picturing herself shaking, hapless, *victimized*. By putting these thoughts down and unraveling her unhelpful self-talk, she gained perspective, recognizing flaws in her thinking. This propelled her toward helpful self-talk:

Situation	Helpful Self-Talk	Feelings	Behavior
Tomorrow I present my marketing proposal to management.	It's a privilege to speak before this group. My boss thinks I have something to offer or I wouldn't be asked to present. I've attended plenty of talks where speakers have said they didn't know an answer but would find it and get back to the questioner. I've never considered them incompetent. That's much better than trying to bluff my way through. I do have valuable information to share and no reason to believe they'd write me off if I can't immediately answer a question or two.	more confident relieved	Prepare the best I can for the talk. Pray for God's help, leave the outcome with him.
	PowerPoint will prompt my memory on what I need to say. If I lose my train of thought I'll read the slide. While this talk offers me a self-introduction to upper management, my career isn't in their hands. It's in God's. I'll ask him to take charge of my mind, tongue, and body language when I speak. I am to prepare as best I can—what's out of my control I leave in his hands. No obstacle is too great for him, not even my blunders. I will do my best and leave the outcome with God.	more in control	Offer to get back to anyone who has a question I can't answer.
	I can deliver the info even with shaky hands or a trembling voice. If I shake, it would be from extra adrenaline, which will diminish if I just accept it and then focus on what I have to say. A few shakes wouldn't be a new experience for my listeners. I've seen plenty of people appear nervous in front of a group. After all, most people aren't comfortable with public speaking. The attendees want to hear my marketing plan, not monitor my nerves.	determined	Accept any adrenaline that flows. Focus on my talk.

Roberta addressed each specific concern with believable thinking. Pronouncements that her presentation would wow everyone, resulting in a next-day promotion, would not have convinced her. No one is guaranteed such success. Instead, she realistically considered her scenario, facing even the worst possible outcome and realizing she could survive it. She also identified ways to cope with the challenge ahead. (If her mind went blank, she would read the slide; if her hands and voice shook, she would accept the adrenaline and focus on the content.) This helpful self-talk would help reduce her stress and optimize her performance.

Focusing on the Future

Anxious thinking is often future-oriented. Anxious self-talk commonly speculates about near or distant events, seeing trouble that rarely materializes. Roberta ruined a week worrying about falling flat when presenting. That never happened—she actually did very well. Evan squandered time for completing his math test, panicked about flunking both that exam and the class. He earned a C on the test and completed high school with no F's on his report card.

Life is not perfect. Bad things do happen. Yet people regularly spoil an otherwise good today worrying about possible trouble tomorrow. Again, Jesus invites us to leave tomorrow with him: "Do not let your hearts be troubled. You believe in God; believe also in me."[5] God gave us minds that enable us to prepare for the future; after we take reasonable and responsible actions, leaving the rest with him offers us comfort and support. Unless we are disaster-relief specialists, focusing on all the terrible things that might happen wastes our energy.

Occasionally fears become reality; God promises to give us the strength we need when that happens. Our lives and our futures are in his hands. We benefit emotionally from trusting him. That is what he wants us to do.

Fearing Change

While some welcome it, many people are unnerved by change. The familiar offers comfort and security to countless individuals.

Some want to hold on to the present because life seems nearly perfect right now. Currently their children, marriage, and business all thrive, and change threatens their happiness. Others are dissatisfied with many aspects of their lives but still dread change. Change introduces the unknown.

Jane feared change. Next month she planned to leave her Arizona home, the only place she'd ever lived, and move to Oregon for her freshman year of college. Originally she looked forward to this step. As the time of departure drew nearer, however, she had second thoughts about choosing to travel so far. Maybe she'd be better off finding a local school.

Before announcing her decision to stay home, she decided to write out her self-talk to discover the source of her anxiety, unraveling each fear.

Situation	Unhelpful Self-Talk	Feelings	Behavior
Soon I leave for my freshman year in Oregon.	I've never lived away from home *which is a problem because* (*WIAPB*) I may really miss my friends and family *BECAUSE* I don't know anyone at college *WIAPB* I'll have no one to talk to if I'm having a tough time *WIAPB* it takes time to build close friendships *WIAPB* no one will understand me *WIAPB* I'll be very lonely *BECAUSE* I'll be all alone *WIAPB* no one else will be in my situation *BECAUSE* it's unusual for freshmen to go away from home for college.	nervous	Lose sleep and appetite.
	I don't know how I'll handle being away from home *BECAUSE* I've never been on my own *WIAPB* I may not like it *BECAUSE* (1) I might not make friends, and (2) I might not be able to handle my classes: (1) I might not make friends *BECAUSE* I don't know how to introduce myself to others and show an interest in them. (2) I might not be able to handle my classes *BECAUSE* they might be too hard *BECAUSE* I may fail to learn the material *BECAUSE* there will be no one available to help me if I have trouble.	insecure	
	I may be better off at a local school *BECAUSE* I'm familiar with things here *which is important because* (*WIIB*) I'd be more comfortable *WIIB* I'll have a better college experience *BECAUSE* I won't be missing home	reluctant	Look into local colleges —avoid going away.

Situation	Unhelpful Self-Talk	Feelings	Behavior
	WIIB I couldn't get over missing home if I went away *BECAUSE* people can't adjust to and enjoy new places and experiences.		

The unknown frightened Jane. She felt vulnerable venturing out of her familiar, secure environment. While she could pass up this particular move, though, she knew that change is unavoidable eventually. After much consideration, she resolved that she would face her fears; she sought to muster the courage to move forward and follow through with her planned adventure.

Situation	Helpful Self-Talk	Feelings	Behavior
Soon I leave for my freshman year in Oregon.	I'm eighteen and have limited life experience. I'll miss out on so much if I decide not to try anything new. Freshmen regularly go away for college and all of them are facing the unknown. It's also common to arrive on campus not knowing other students. This is a great opportunity—so many will be open to new friendships. I can introduce myself and show interest in those I meet. It's unlikely I won't find anyone I enjoy or relate to. College orientation is designed in part to help students get to know each other. In fact, the schedule suggests we'll be so busy for a while that I may not have time to feel lonely.	confident excited optimistic	Stick with my plans. Be friendly and outgoing in meeting new people once I arrive.
	I was accepted because admissions thought I could do the work. If I have trouble I can talk to classmates, make an appointment with the professor, or see what student services might be available to help. I wouldn't be the first college student who needed a little academic assistance.		Ask for help if I have academic difficulties.
	I'm sure I'll miss home sometimes, like everyone else, but I can talk to people at school, get involved in activities there, or occasionally call home. I can also read my Bible, pray, and find a church to attend. Just as he is now, Christ will remain my constant companion as I embrace this new opportunity. Going away to college is a privilege and an adventure that I will take with him at my side each step of the way.		Pray, read the Bible, find a church—stay close to Christ.

"Jesus Christ is the same yesterday and today and forever."[6] He is the one single constant in our lives; *everything* else changes, and no one escapes this. Focusing on Christ's continuous presence and help offers us security through all time and all circumstances.

General Scary Statements

One last notable type of anxious thought is the general scary statement. Anxious people often expect to be unhinged by unspecified future trouble. Not wanting to tread near such discomfort, they make broad statements, such as "I couldn't handle chairing a committee," or "I'd feel awkward attending a concert alone," and stop right there. They never challenge the credibility of those assumptions but quickly, unquestioningly accept them as truth.

Carmen thought in broad strokes when she considered hosting dinner guests. She simply told herself she could not bear the stress of entertaining in her home. This self-talk produced a feeling of anxiety and behaviors of avoidance—she never invited company for dinner. Refusing to prepare a meal for friends affected her social life, though. Her friends welcomed her into their homes, and she knew it was her "turn." When writing her unhelpful self-talk about this situation, "because" and "which is a problem because" challenged her general scary thinking, diminishing the intensity of her fear in the process.

Situation	Unhelpful Self-Talk	Feelings	Behavior
Considering inviting friends over for dinner.	I'd be nervous fixing dinner for my friends *BECAUSE* the meal might not turn out well *BECAUSE* the meat might be raw or dry and the vegetables overcooked *which is a problem because* (*WIAPB*) my friends would think I'm a terrible cook *WIAPB* they'd have less respect for me *BECAUSE* they'd think I'm incompetent in the kitchen *WIAPB* they may end our friendship *BECAUSE* they wouldn't stay friends with someone who serves disappointing food.	insecure	Don't invite.
	Conversation may not flow *WIAPB* there could be awkward silences *BECAUSE* sometimes this happens when we're together *WIAPB* I'll be responsible for giving everyone a fun evening *WIAPB* I won't be	full of dread	

Situation	Unhelpful Self-Talk	Feelings	Behavior
	able to think of interesting things to say *WIAPB* my friends may just endure it *BECAUSE* they'll sit passively and expect me to entertain them *WIAPB* everyone will hate the evening *WIAPB* they'll look down on me *BECAUSE* I hosted such a miserable party *WIAPB* what others think of me determines my worth.		

When Carmen got specific she realized her stress was the product of unchallenged beliefs about impressing her friends. Unraveling the problem-thinking uncovered the ridiculous thought that they might abandon her over a lousy meal and a dull conversation. Breaking down general scary statements led her to a more helpful interpretation.

Situation	Helpful Self-Talk	Feelings	Behavior
Consider-ing invit-ing friends over for dinner.	It boils down to pride. I'm nervous about fixing dinner for my friends because I want them to be impressed with my culinary skills. But that would not be the purpose of the evening. They would come to my home to eat a meal while visiting together. We enjoy each other's company. I'll pick something easy to fix and if the meal doesn't taste good, it wouldn't be a new trauma for anybody. Everyone has eaten a bad meal, and everyone who cooks occasionally fails in their efforts. Who would end a friendship over subpar food?	resolved assured more secure	Invite. Select a menu easy to prepare. Identify some pos-sible con-versational topics in advance of the evening.
	I can be prepared with a few conversational top-ics. Usually my friends like to talk and we have a good time. If people are lifeless that night I can suggest a game. All that's in my control is to plan an evening I think we'll enjoy. The outcome is out of my control. I can't make others put forth effort. If they don't and the evening's a downer, again, we've endured that before. Our friendships have survived lackluster evenings together. My pride can survive it too. My worth comes from Christ alone—not from others or my ability to entertain well.		Plan games to have avail-able if con-versation wanes.

In her helpful self-talk, Carmen solved any problems that weren't dissolved simply by unraveling her general scary thoughts. She would prepare a simple meal, plan some topics in advance, and have games ready in case people had little to say. The reminder that only Christ holds power over her value freed her to risk serving a tasteless meal to a group of people bored to tears with the party she hosted! On the other hand, she recognized the more likely possibility of a fun evening with her friends.

Separating the Inside-Our-Control From the Outside-Our-Control

There is a saying that has become very widely known as the "Serenity Prayer," some words for which were spoken in a 1943 sermon by the theologian Reinhold Niebuhr, and one version of which reads:

> God, give us grace to accept with serenity
> the things that cannot be changed,
> Courage to change the things
> that should be changed,
> and the Wisdom to distinguish
> the one from the other.

We reduce anxiety when we identify what is inside our control to improve life for ourselves and others, act on those opportunities, and then leave with God what is outside our control. People waste much time and energy fretting over what they cannot influence. Jesus addressed this common practice, asking, "Who of you by worrying can add a single hour to your life? Since you cannot do this very little thing, why do you worry about the rest?"[7] He instructs us to let go of what we cannot change and trust him.

The Seven Steps facilitate recognition of what's inside and outside your control. When you include in the helpful self-talk specific plans to act on what you can, leaving the rest with

Christ, you increase the power of the self-talk to relieve emotional distress.

When intimidated about entertaining friends, Carmen noted that she could select something easy to prepare, plan ahead with some talking topics, and have a few games ready just in case; the rest she would leave with God.

Roberta turned around her fear of a disastrous performance in front of head honchos by identifying variables inside her control. She would prepare as best she could, promise to get back to anyone with the requested information should she be stumped by a question, look to PowerPoint if she lost track, focus on what she had to share rather than on her shaking hands or trembling voice, and pray for God's help. Everything else she would leave with him.

In his effort to combat test anxiety, Evan observed that "What's in my control now is to use my time to read through the exam and try my best. I can do that. The outcome I leave with Christ." Learning to quickly respond to anxiety by identifying and acting on what's in our control and leaving the rest with God can spare us significant suffering.

Coping With Multiple Stressors: The I/O Exercise

Have you ever felt bombarded with so many problems that you froze in your tracks, so overwhelmed you could neither think nor move? Separating what is in your control from what is out of your control is useful both when facing a single challenge and when confronting multiple stressors at once. But when many threats hit concurrently, writing self-talk about each issue may not be realistic. In such circumstances the Seven Steps require too much time, adding to your stress. The "Inside My Control/ Outside My Control Exercise," or "I/O Exercise" (listed without comment in appendix C), works better to diffuse anxiety when numerous concerns loom.

———————

Melanie's mind raced as she arrived home from the office on Tuesday evening. Many pressures overwhelmed her. After yelling at family members four times in as many minutes, she thought of the I/O Exercise. She felt she could not afford the forty-five minutes necessary to implement the tool, yet after an hour of spinning her wheels and snapping repeatedly, she was convinced otherwise. The time investment was needed. Both she and her husband, Troy, worked full time and strove to keep up with the demands of raising three teenagers. No surprise that occasionally these and other stressors consumed her. The I/O Exercise would help her reclaim control of her life.

I/O Exercise

Action 1: List each of your worries/stresses.

Be very specific. For example, it's too general to say, "My kids are absolutely impossible." Instead, record each problem you encounter with them, like disrespectful talk, ignoring parental direction, failing in school, or making bad choices in friends. Leave many blank lines between each concern and space for a column to be added on the left side of the paper at action 3.

Sitting down to identify precise sources of distress, Melanie noted:

I/O Exercise

---

1. We're carrying a $10,000 credit card balance, getting bigger every month. I don't see how we'll be able to pay it off.

2. At parent/teacher conferences last night, we learned Hunter is failing history and earning a D in math and English.

I/O Exercise

3. A big project is due at work on Friday.

   A. I don't completely understand what my boss wants.

   B. I don't have enough time to complete the project.

4. My sister and her family arrive Friday to spend the weekend.

   A. The house needs cleaning.

   B. I need to plan menus for their visit.

   C. Groceries must be purchased.

   D. I have no idea how to entertain our guests on Saturday.

Action 2: Review each worry and list what's "Inside My Control" ("I") to solve. Also identify what's "Outside My Control" ("O") about the issue.

Again, be very specific.

Melanie brainstormed and jotted down every option that came to mind for resolving her concerns. She also stated what was out of her control.

I/O Exercise

I = Inside My Control   **O = Outside My Control**

1. We're carrying a $10,000 credit card balance, getting bigger every month. I don't see how we'll be able to pay it off.

   I: Plan with Troy to stop charging. Cut up the cards.

   I: Record all expenditures for a month; see what we can cut.

   I: Agree on a budget, including a savings plan, and stick to it.

   I: Put cash in envelopes monthly for each area of spending; when the money is gone, it's gone.

   I: Look for second jobs to help pay off our debt.

   I: Search for the lowest possible interest rate(s) for our debt.

   O: The past—the fact that we now owe this money

   O: Unexpected future emergencies that require spending

I/O Exercise
I = Inside My Control   O = Outside My Control

2. At parent/teacher conferences last night, we learned Hunter is failing history and earning a D in math and English.

I: Make plan with Troy to talk with Hunter about the need to invest time and effort to get a good education. Discuss self-discipline; identify how he'd benefit from developing more.

I: Tell Hunter he must begin his homework thirty minutes after arriving home from school. Monitor him more closely on this.

I: Allow no electronic communication while doing homework—choose with him a quiet place to study with minimal distraction.

I: Have Hunter complete homework before any evening free time—check to see that this happens as much as possible.

I: Check in weekly or biweekly with teachers to make sure he is keeping up with assignments and earning all passing grades.

I: Identify consequences for not keeping up with schoolwork.

O: Whether or not Hunter improves performance after doing all "I's"

O: His reaction to plan after we've discussed it respectfully

3. A big project is due at work on Friday.

A. I don't completely understand what my boss wants.

I: Write down questions to ask boss about the project.

I: Make an appointment with boss to ask the questions.

I: Ask co-workers with more related experience for guidance.

O: My boss's availability and willingness to help

O: Difficulty of the project

O: Co-workers' knowledge of the project/willingness to help

B. I don't have enough time to complete the project.

I: Work one evening at home on this.

I: Block off work time during which I won't take calls.

O: How long it takes to complete the project

O: Boss's reaction/how project turns out after doing my best

4. My sister and her family arrive Friday to spend the weekend.

A. The house needs cleaning.

I: Clean it myself.

I/O Exercise
I = Inside My Control   O = Outside My Control

> **I:** Assign some chores to Troy, some to the kids.
>
> **I:** Hire someone to clean.
>
> **I:** Leave the house a mess.
>
> **O:** Other demands on the family's time
>
> **O:** Family's reaction to my delegating this task

B. I need to plan menus for their visit.

> **I:** Set aside time to plan out meals.
>
> **I:** Get ideas from Troy and kids on what to serve.
>
> **O:** How the meals turn out once I've done my best
>
> **O:** Whether our guests like the food they're served

C. Groceries must be purchased.

> **I:** Set aside time to go to the grocery store.
>
> **I:** Ask Troy to go on Thursday.
>
> **O:** Troy's schedule

D. I have no idea how to entertain our guests on Saturday.

> **I:** Ask Troy/kids for ideas of what we might do Saturday.
>
> **I:** Look online to see what will be going on in our area.
>
> **I:** Identify several options to propose; let guests decide.
>
> **O:** What's happening in our area this weekend
>
> **O:** How much everyone enjoys what we choose to do

Action 3: Decide which of the "I's" you will actually do. Then prioritize them, considering the entire group of "I's" that you selected. Write beside each its number of priority.

(For example, if you decided to address eight of your "I's," you would rank your priorities one through eight.)

Next, Melanie reviewed all the "I's" regarding each stress she identified. Understanding that she need not exercise every available option, she decided which "I's" to implement, selecting twenty-three of the twenty-eight listed. Then, in the left column, she assigned each chosen action a priority ranking.

Priority	I/O Exercise I = Inside My Control O = Outside My Control
	1. We're carrying a $10,000 credit card balance, getting bigger every month. I don't see how we'll be able to pay it off.
18	**I:** Plan with Troy to stop charging. Cut up the cards.
20	**I:** Record all expenditures for a month; see what we can cut.
22	**I:** Agree on a budget, including a savings plan, and stick to it.
23	**I:** Put cash in envelopes monthly for each area of spending; when the money is gone, it's gone.
	I: Look for second jobs to help pay off our debt.
19	**I:** Search for the lowest possible interest rate(s) for our debt.
	O: The past—the fact that we now owe this money
	O: Unexpected future emergencies that require spending
	2. At parent/teacher conferences last night, we learned Hunter is failing history and earning a D in math and English.
1	**I:** Make plan with Troy to talk with Hunter about the need to invest time and effort to get a good education. Discuss self-discipline; identify how he'd benefit from developing more.
2	**I:** Tell Hunter he must begin his homework thirty minutes after arriving home from school. Monitor him more closely on this.
3	**I:** Allow no electronic communication while doing homework—choose with him a quiet place to study with minimal distraction.
10	**I:** Have Hunter complete homework before any evening free time—check to see that this happens as much as possible.
21	**I:** Check in weekly or biweekly with teachers to make sure he is keeping up with assignments and earning all passing grades.
4	**I:** Identify consequences for not keeping up with schoolwork.
	O: Whether Hunter improves performance after doing all "I's"
	O: His reaction to plan after we've discussed it respectfully
	3. A big project is due at work on Friday.
	A. I don't completely understand what my boss wants.

Priority	I/O Exercise I = Inside My Control O = Outside My Control
9	**I:** Write down questions to ask boss about the project.
11	**I:** Make an appointment with boss to ask the questions.
12	**I:** Ask co-workers with more related experience for guidance.
	O: My boss's availability and willingness to help
	O: Difficulty of the project
	O: Co-workers' knowledge of the project/willingness to help
	B. I don't have enough time to complete the project.
14	**I:** Work one evening at home on this.
13	**I:** Block off work time during which I won't take calls.
	O: How long it takes to complete the project
	O: Boss's reaction/how project turns out after doing my best
	4. My sister and her family arrive Friday to spend the weekend.
	A. The house needs cleaning.
	I: Clean it myself.
5	**I:** Assign some chores to Troy, some to the kids.
	I: Hire someone to clean.
	I: Leave the house a mess.
	O: Other demands on the family's time
	O: Family's reaction to my delegating this task
	B. I need to plan menus for their visit.
6	**I:** Set aside time to plan out meals.
7	**I:** Get ideas from Troy and kids on what to serve.
	O: How the meals turn out once I've done my best
	O: Whether our guests like the food they're served
	C. Groceries must be purchased.
	I: Set aside time to go to the grocery store.
8	**I:** Ask Troy to go on Thursday.
	O: Troy's schedule
	D. I have no idea how to entertain our guests on Saturday.

Priority	I/O Exercise I = Inside My Control O = Outside My Control
16	**I:** Ask Troy/kids for ideas of what we might do Saturday.
15	**I:** Look online to see what will be going on in our area.
17	**I:** Identify several options to propose; let guests decide.
	O: What's happening in our area this weekend
	O: How much everyone enjoys what we choose to do

Action 4: Take out your calendar and decide precisely when you'll address each priority.

Set reasonable goals. Write the dates on your planner according to the order you chose. And be sure to leave yourself time for the unexpected.

Melanie looked at her calendar and recorded when she hoped to deal with every priority. She set aside more time than she thought each would require; scheduling herself too tightly would only add to her pressure. Unrealistic expectations could set her up to fall short and dissolve in stress when surprise demands intruded. She jotted down some specific times for initiating duties only to help her determine what she could sensibly complete each day. Over the next eight days she would attend to her first twenty-one priorities, some of which involved new practices she hoped to continue indefinitely. (See next page.)

Melanie decided to address priorities 22 and 23 in May:

May

Mon

> 15
>
> [22] Discuss budget with Troy. Agree on plan.
>
> [23] Start envelope spending plan with Troy?

April

Tues	Wed	Thurs	Fri	Sat	Sun	Mon	Tues
11	12	13	14	15	16	17	18
7 p.m.:	8 a.m.:	7 p.m.:	6 p.m.:	Guests here	Guests leave in afternoon	9 p.m.:	Noon:
[1] [2] [3] [4]	[11] [12] [13]	[15] [16] [17]	Guests arrive			[18] [19] [20]	[21]
Hunter talk	Schedule meeting, ask for help, block off time.	Search for Sat. options & get ideas from fam., select options				Talk w/ Troy re. cards; cut up if he agrees, find lower rates, start records	Check w/ teacher & set up regular checks on H's status.
8 p.m.:	7–9 p.m.:	7:30–9:30 p.m.:					
[5] [6] [7] [8] [9] [10]	[14]	[17A]					
Assign, plan, get ideas, ask T, write project Qs, & check on H.	Work project	Clean house with fam.					

Action 5: *When you catch yourself worrying about any of the "I's," remind yourself: you have a plan for dealing with each.*

You need only focus on your first priority, as the others will be taken care of as detailed on your calendar. Therefore, you can let go of thinking about all but your first priority listed.

Melanie regularly tied herself in knots by contemplating all her tasks simultaneously. This also blurred her focus on her current assignment, as she tried to hold in her head the many items awaiting her that she dare not forget. Writing a specific and reasonable plan for accomplishing everything freed her to attend only to her present priority. The written plan both reduced her stress and enabled her to operate more efficiently.

Action 6: *When concerns about an "O" cross your mind, remind yourself: no amount of worry will in any way alter its outcome.*

If something is truly outside your control, then fretting, manipulating, planning, maneuvering, and losing sleep thinking about it will not change it. So when you find yourself thinking about the "O's," pray about them and leave them in God's hands. Then focus your energy on the next "I."

Melanie wasted countless time and energy worrying about what she could not change. After this exercise, she determined that anytime she worried about her boss's availability, meals for this weekend, or money foolishly spent last year, she'd pray about her concern, leave her burden with Christ, then focus on how to improve life today. Quickly leaving with God what's out of our control is a mental discipline that benefits everyone who practices it.

Recognizing Classic Anxious Behaviors

One primary behavior associated with anxiety is avoidance. When we avoid what frightens us, fear grows. The longer we stay away from what we dread, the bigger the threat becomes. For example, those who fear flying increase their anxiety by avoiding travel on planes for years. Yet simply making one-self fly without choosing helpful self-talk to interpret all that happens with air travel—"white-knuckling it" through the ordeal—may reap few rewards, potentially even increasing the fear. Helpful self-talk needs to accompany bold steps to face our fears. When we simultaneously take charge of the two factors inside our control—behavior and self-talk—we can reduce anxiety.

Sadly, those who allow fear to dominate their lives unintentionally end up in a prison of more and more restrictions. People who fear traveling far away sometimes permit that fear to dictate their behavior, and their worlds gradually shrink until they feel comfortable only in their local communities. Certainly we need not face down every potential threat (for example, people can enjoy full lives without overcoming a fear of skydiving or swimming with sharks). But many miss wonderful opportunities or fail to correct problems that hurt themselves and others because they avoid what frightens them.

Angela let fear direct her behavior. Dreading the thought of an angry or even rejecting daughter, she avoided disciplining Dominique. Dominique seemed oblivious to this vulnerability in her mother, until recently. She just got her driver's license and, before long, yielded to the temptations this new freedom afforded her. Angela's self-talk reveals her hesitancy to impose consequences on Dominique after discovering her problem behavior.

Situation	Unhelpful Self-Talk	Feelings	Behavior
Just caught Dominique in several lies.	I let Dominique use the car *BECAUSE* I believed she'd just pick up her friends and go to the movie *BECAUSE* she promised she would *which is a problem because* (*WIAPB*) she lied to me *WIAPB* she used to be trustworthy but now she's turning into a typical teen *BECAUSE* she's breaking the rules *WIAPB* I can't monitor her all the time *WIAPB* there's no point in trying *BECAUSE* teens will be teens.	perplexed	Avoid confronting— ignore bad behavior.
	I heard she was drinking at that party *WIAPB* she sees no problem with this *WIAPB* she won't listen to me *BECAUSE* she thinks I don't understand *BECAUSE* I'm not of her generation *WIAPB* there's nothing I can do *BECAUSE* teens never listen to parents.	doubtful	
	If I confront and give her a consequence she'll get mad at me *BECAUSE* she doesn't like being told what to do *WIAPB* she'll hold it against me *WIAPB* she will distance from me *WIAPB* our relationship will be strained *WIAPB* I want to enjoy a strong bond with her *BECAUSE* it's so much more comfortable *which is important BECAUSE* (*WIIB*) I hate conflict *WIIB* I shouldn't have to deal with conflict.	intimidated	

Angela's unhelpful self-talk rationalized caving in to her fears, thereby avoiding her duty to deal with her daughter's lies and underage drinking. Helpful self-talk empowered her to parent Dominique responsibly.

Situation	Helpful Self-Talk	Feelings	Behavior
Just caught Dominique in several lies.	I am disappointed in Dominique but glad I discovered her lies so I can nip this in the bud. It's not uncommon for teens to test the boundaries, but that doesn't mean she has to reject all our standards. She knows right from wrong. I can talk with her about what happened, the risks involved for her, and why I'll monitor her more closely till trust is restored. The burden's on her to prove herself to me.	empowered determined confident	Confront in a firm but respectful manner. Listen to her while exploring with her the reasoning that led to her bad choices.
	She made a number of bad choices we need to review. She was not to be at the party at all. If she'd obeyed, she wouldn't have been drinking. This is a perfect time to help her develop more of an internal		

Situation	Helpful Self-Talk	Feelings	Behavior
	locus of control, whatever her temptations. Teens may protest listening to parents, but studies show no one has more influence over them. I need to be an active parent and deal with the problem.		Choose a logical consequence and follow through.
	I won't let anticipated anger intimidate me into neglecting my responsibility as a parent. I don't need to yell. I will talk reasonably about what happened and discuss a logical consequence. She needs a parent more than a friend. If she is disrespectful in response I'll deal with that directly as well. Allowing her to use threats of anger to get her way would foster a manipulative style that can't be allowed to take root in her. Hating conflict is no excuse for shirking my duties as a parent.		

Avoidance combined with scary thinking increases anxiety. If Angela repeatedly ignores her daughter's unacceptable choices, dishonest and risky behavior more likely becomes the teen's norm. Angela then silently worries and agonizes as she watches Dominique go further down a dangerous path of rebellion. Turning around entrenched erroneous behavior is much more difficult than correcting bad decisions as soon as they emerge. Choosing helpful self-talk emboldens us to stop avoiding and squarely face what needs to be addressed. Such choices ultimately diminish our anxiety and offer relief.

Employing Relationships to Overcome Anxiety

Continuing the focus throughout this book on three types of relationships—between thoughts, feelings, and behaviors; with Jesus Christ; and with people—let's examine how each can help us take charge of anxiety.

The Relationship Between Thoughts, Feelings, and Behaviors

We've already considered how anxiety thrives on general scary statements. Writing out the Seven Steps when worry involves one issue, or the I/O Exercise when multiple stresses hit at once, helps us move beyond generalities and precisely define fear. Specificity alone often reduces anxiety. The following two Rules for Living remind people to push for specifics as soon as they sense apprehension brewing inside:

Rules for Living

1. I do not get to be afraid unless I can identify a real and specific threat.
2. If a real and specific threat exists, I'll determine what I can and cannot control about it. Then I'll ask God to guide and strengthen me as I act on what's in my control and leave with him what's out of my control.

Monitor your thoughts and behaviors. Recognize scary, frightening interpretations and avoidant conduct. If these anxiety-producing practices have become your style, write out your self-talk once a day with the goal of automatically interpreting life in a helpful way at least 90 percent of the time. This will probably require about a month of writing for about thirty minutes a day (see "The Relationship Between Thoughts, Feelings, and Behaviors" at end of chapter 8 for a more in-depth discussion). Simultaneously, tolerate no more avoidant behaviors regarding issues that you truly need to address. Remember, when you take charge of your thoughts and your behaviors you can build new connections in your brain and find emotional relief.

A Relationship With Jesus Christ

"Fear not!" is a phrase frequently repeated in the Bible. God obviously understands our human tendency to worry. He also instructs us to put our faith and confidence in him, offering everyone an option infinitely more potent than merely letting go of threats we cannot change.

Chapter 5 considered how Christ invites us to leave with him—the all-knowing, all-loving, all-powerful Creator of the universe—what's outside of our control. He is not a genie who grants our every wish, yet he promises us the strength to deal with any challenge and that he will never abandon us. Keeping our eyes focused on Christ through whatever we encounter offers supernatural peace and confidence *within* the storm. He takes us outside the box of this world's perils and grants us ultimate security with him.

Reading words of comfort from God can help soothe fear. Here are some verses that may relieve your anxiety. Remember when you read the Bible to record passages that especially speak to you.

> The LORD is my light and my salvation—
>   whom shall I fear?
> The LORD is the stronghold of my life—
>   of whom shall I be afraid?[8]

> The righteous cry out, and the LORD hears them;
>   he delivers them from all their troubles.
> The LORD is close to the brokenhearted
>   and saves those who are crushed in spirit.[9]

> [He says,] "Be still, and know that I am God."[10]

> When I am afraid, I put my trust in you.[11]

> Truly my soul finds rest in God;
>   my salvation comes from him.
> Truly he is my rock and my salvation;
>   he is my fortress, I will never be shaken. . . .
> Trust in him at all times, you people;
>   pour out your hearts to him,
>   for God is our refuge.[12]

> Whoever dwells in the shelter of the Most High
>   will rest in the shadow of the Almighty.

I will say of the LORD, "He is my refuge and my
    fortress,
    my God, in whom I trust."
Surely he will save you
    from the fowler's snare
    and from the deadly pestilence.
He will cover you with his feathers,
    and under his wings you will find refuge;
    his faithfulness will be your shield and rampart.[13]

I lift up my eyes to the mountains—
    where does my help come from?
My help comes from the LORD,
    the Maker of heaven and earth.[14]

So do not fear, for I am with you;
    do not be dismayed, for I am your God.
I will strengthen you and help you;
    I will uphold you with my righteous right hand.[15]

"Peace I [Jesus] leave with you; my peace I give to you. I do not give to you as the world gives. Do not let your hearts be troubled and do not be afraid."[16]

"I [Jesus] have told you these things, so that in me you may have peace. In this world you will have trouble. But take heart! I have overcome the world."[17]

If God is for us, who can be against us?[18]

Do not be anxious about anything, but in every situation, by prayer and petition, with thanksgiving, present your requests to God. And the peace of God, which transcends all understanding, will guard your hearts and your minds in Christ Jesus.[19]

The Spirit God gave us does not make us timid, but gives us power, love and self-discipline.[20]

Devotional books can help us find relief from anxiety as well, by focusing our thoughts on Christ. Sarah Young's *Jesus Calling* offers brief words of reassurance for each day of the year, reminding us of his presence and involvement in our lives no matter what challenges we face.

Human Relationships

Relationships with people can diminish anxiety too. For a number of reasons, scary thoughts that torment us when hidden in the dark recesses of our mind often lose power when verbalized to trusted family or friends. Sharing our fears with others may provide us with a different and less-threatening perspective on our situation. Additionally, other people might suggest new and better strategies for dealing with our problems. A further benefit of opening up to family or friends is the relief that often comes from knowing that another person understands our struggle.

The apostle Paul proclaimed,

> Praise be to the God and Father of our Lord Jesus Christ, the Father of compassion and the God of all comfort, who comforts us in all our troubles, so that we can comfort those in any trouble with the comfort we ourselves receive from God.[21]

God equips his followers to minister to those in distress. Christians are instructed to pray for and assist those in difficult circumstances. God's plan is for people to play a significant role in easing one another's anxiety.

10

Conquering Anger

In your anger do not sin.[1]

Kyle's temper flares at any irritation. His wife and children regularly walk on eggshells, trying to avoid setting off Dad, who verbally attacks them in response to the slightest provocation. Co-workers consider him hot-headed, and his boss has warned him twice in the last month to keep his cool.

Driving the freeway, Kyle routinely yells and curses at other drivers. Their rudeness and stupidity never cease to amaze him. The following self-talk typifies his automatic thinking on the road.

Situation	Unhelpful Self-Talk	Feelings	Behavior
I've seen "Merge Right" signs for miles, inching ahead in bumper-	She darted in *BECAUSE* she's a self-centered idiot *BECAUSE* she refused to wait in line like everyone else *BECAUSE* she can get by with it *which is a problem because* (*WIAPB*) I've spent all this time in line and she hasn't *WIAPB* now she's ahead of me *WIAPB* she doesn't deserve it *WIAPB* it's not fair *WIAPB* life should be fair.	outraged	Tailgate. Try to pass once we're out of the bottle-

179

Situation	Unhelpful Self-Talk	Feelings	Behavior
to-bumper traffic. A driver who waited to merge till the last minute just cut me off.	She squeezed in, last second, *WIAPB* she thinks she pulled one over on me *BECAUSE* she didn't bother waiting like I did *WIAPB* she's gloating *BECAUSE* I know what she's thinking *BECAUSE* I can read minds.	provoked	neck; stare her down with a nasty look.
	She had no right to do this *WIAPB* I'm not letting it go *BECAUSE* I don't have to *BECAUSE* I'll show her *which is important because* (*WIIB*) my manhood is at risk *BECAUSE* I let someone ace me out *WIAPB* real men don't let others push them around *BECAUSE* real men always win.	vengeful vulnerable[2]	

Many people associate anger with Kyle's out-of-control words and actions and feel uncomfortable with this particular emotion. Some feel guilty when they experience anger, even denying its presence in their emotional repertoire. Many of us have learned to tell ourselves, "Anger is bad," and yet Jesus, the Christian's guide for living, clearly knew anger. Outraged at the desecration of the temple, Jesus cast out the moneychangers, brandishing a whip and overturning their tables.[3] He also experienced anger toward the Pharisees.[4] Clearly he was not always kind and gentle or meek and mild.

Righteous anger motivates people to take action to improve life around them—to fight child abuse and corruption, for example. Feeling angry is neither wrong nor unchristian. What can cause trouble is *toxic anger*, which, says psychologist and anger specialist W. Doyle Gentry, "is distinguished from both annoyance and normal, nontoxic anger by its frequency, intensity and/or duration."[5] Toxic anger is "anger that is experienced by otherwise normal people much too frequently, is too intense, and[/or] lasts too long."[6]

Paul assumed that we do experience anger but directed us to take charge of this emotion. Love, joy, sadness, fear, and anger are basic human feelings. We need not debate whether or not we experience anger—everyone does. Anger is not only unavoidable;

at times it is necessary and positive. The challenge is to follow Paul's instruction: *"In your anger do not sin."*

Harmful Expressions of Anger

Anger can be communicated in destructive ways. Some, like Kyle, engage in verbal tirades involving name calling and putdowns. One mother who had trouble controlling her tongue regularly yelled at her unmotivated sixteen-year-old, "You're a loser! You'll never amount to anything!"

One husband threatened divorce whenever exasperated with his wife, who learned to ignore the outbursts because his language commonly leapt to the extreme.

Tiffany, whose scenario we'll soon evaluate, habitually reacted to frustrating circumstances with rage. When she learned her daughter attended a drinking party, she instantly screamed her intention to impose multiple, difficult-to-enforce punishments (see Angela's story in chapter 9 for an opposite but equally ineffective parental response).

Others inflict the silent treatment when angry, shutting down and emotionally withdrawing to punish the person with whom they're upset. Whenever Lisa was disgusted with her husband she refused to speak to him for days. He could not force her to engage with him, and she privately derived great satisfaction from seeing him squirm under oppressive silence.

Sarcasm can provide yet another potentially damaging means of expressing anger. While this communication device may be employed in harmless, witty, instructive, and even delightful ways, at other times it simply permits people to deliver angry messages without owning their content.

Brittany repeatedly hid her rage under the socially acceptable cover of sarcasm, protecting her vulnerable inner being behind its tough, angry shell. She rarely confronted people straightforwardly, instead expressing bitter dissatisfaction through humor. If recipients protested her thinly veiled barbs, she'd coolly ask, "Can't you take a joke?" Adults felt manipulated by her sarcasm, and her twisted remarks thoroughly confused and pained her kids. Her third-grader, who struggled in school, had no clue how to interpret the caustic "I'm so proud of you!" in response to the F she got on her spelling test.

Avoiding Destructive Anger

We need not engage in destructive rage. We can take action to cope with anger in a healthy way by objectively reviewing the situation to which we're reacting and identifying any issues of our own that might create unnecessary or excessive anger. Sometimes a healthy resolution involves confronting the other person. We can more wisely decide whether or not to confront if we first consider who that person is and then anticipate how he or she might respond. When this seems our best choice, "Gentle Confrontations" (see next main section below) provide a framework for addressing grievances with others.

Action 1: Examine the Situation

To take charge of anger, we must first acknowledge its presence. We cannot control what we deny exists. Next, we need to identify the source of our animosity and determine whether this is righteous anger or an unnecessary irritation we could quickly dismiss. Objectively examining the situation helps us understand our frustration.

Does this sound familiar? The first of the Seven Steps is "Describe the Situation" (see chapter 2), which involves recording only the facts of what's happening. After discerning precisely what transpired, we can recognize our interpretation of the events by identifying the self-talk that created the anger.

This chapter opened with Kyle, who regularly struggled with rage. When he used the Seven Steps, first describing objectively his situation on the freeway and later (step 3) uncovering his unhelpful reaction, he recognized the foolishness of wasting such energy over a momentary delay and vowed to employ the following helpful self-talk next time someone cut in front of him.

Situation	Helpful Self-Talk	Feelings	Behavior
I've seen "Merge Right" signs for miles, inching ahead in bumper-to-bumper traffic. A driver who waited to merge till the last minute just cut me off.	She darted in front of me. I don't like that she didn't merge earlier, but a lot of people are rude and pushy. It's aggravating, but life's not fair. I can't control her. So she set me back a car's length—in the big scheme, a few seconds' delay doesn't matter. I waste much more than that every day.	determined	Turn on radio, listen to music.
	I can't read minds. I don't know that she's proud of cutting me off. It's a waste of time to speculate on what I don't know and can't find out, and what she thinks is out of my control.	more relaxed	
	"Showing her" is not an option. Vehicles must be operated responsibly or someone could get hurt. It's time I learn to deal with frustration. A "real man" doesn't always need to assert dominance. Only an insecure man has to prove himself whenever it seems someone steps on his toes. Let it go. This is no big deal.	in control confident	Drive responsibly.

Kyle was determined to resolve his anger through thinking differently. Writing the Seven Steps enables people to understand the thinking that creates their anger. Such knowledge then helps them decide whether to use helpful self-talk to simply let go of it or to confront the source of their irritation.

Tiffany also routinely interpreted life in an anger-producing manner. She characteristically flew into a rage when she learned that her daughter, Natasha, lied to her and attended a party where she and other teens drank beer. Review Tiffany's unhelpful self-talk to understand the thinking that fed her anger.

Situation	Unhelpful Self-Talk	Feelings	Behavior
I just caught Natasha in a number of lies.	I let her go out with her friends *BECAUSE* she said they'd go to the mall *which is a problem because* (*WIAPB*) she looked in my eyes and promised (*WIAPB*) she purposely lied *BECAUSE* she thought she could get away with it *WIAPB* she took advantage of me *WIAPB* if Tina's mom hadn't inadvertently told me I'd have never found out *WIAPB* I wonder what else Natasha's doing that I don't know *BECAUSE* if she could lie about this she could lie about anything *WIAPB* she'll never be honest or trustworthy *BECAUSE* teens who lie once end up delinquents.	manipulated deceived	Scream. Give excessive conse-quences that won't be enforced, including grounding her for the next six
	I heard she was drinking *WIAPB* she sees no problem with that *WIAPB* she thinks she can get by with anything *BECAUSE* she's blatantly disobeying me *WIAPB* I'll make her pay for this *BECAUSE* she has blown my trust *WIAPB* I'll never let her out of my sight again!	furious	months with no access to electronics.

Contrary to Kyle's circumstances, Tiffany's situation required more than new thinking to find relief from her anger. She had a responsibility to confront her daughter's unacceptable behavior. Tiffany must take action.

But she must control herself when dealing with Natasha. Otherwise, she (not Natasha) would become the issue, and her parental respect and authority would be diminished in her daughter's eyes. She needed to remember that Natasha had never before defied her like this; she was hardly a juvenile delinquent. Yet she also ought to face a consequence that would seriously discourage her from repeating this bad choice in the future.

Situation	Helpful Self-Talk	Feelings	Behavior
I just caught Natasha in a number of lies.	I'm angry that she lied to me and engaged in risky behavior. It's true that my trust in her is shaken. Now I know she's capable of lying to me. She needs to grasp the implications of her choice. If I yell at her, her defenses will go up and she won't take in what I say. I can sit down and talk with her about what happened, the risks involved for her, and why I'll have to monitor her closely until trust is restored. The burden	in control patient determined	Confront firmly but respectfully. Listen to her while exploring with her the reasoning

184

Situation	Helpful Self-Talk	Feelings	Behavior
	is on her to prove herself to me. She's a good girl who's made many good choices. It's common for teens to test boundaries, but that doesn't mean they're lost.		that led to her bad choice.
	If she'd kept her word she would have stayed away from the party and from alcohol. That blatant disobedience must be stopped. This is an important teaching moment. If I verbally attack her, my anger will be the focus instead of her actions. If I'm out of control I'll also threaten extreme consequences that I'll never keep. Then I'll lose my credibility and she'll more likely repeat her mistake. I need to explore with her how to have an internal locus of control, whatever temptations cross her path. I'll choose a logical consequence.		Give a logical consequence and follow through. Monitor her more closely until she shows she's trustworthy.

Kyle and Tiffany had hot tempers. Writing self-talk helped them get perspective and directed each toward resolving the anger either on their own through helpful self-talk or by confronting the person with whom they were upset. Writing self-talk offers us clarity when we experience anger. After objectively identifying the issue and our interpretation that created anger, two important questions can help us decide whether or not to confront:

- Are any of my own issues creating excessive anger?
- With whom am I angry?

Action 2: *Know Yourself*

Before confronting others, we are wise to examine ourselves and determine why we're so upset. Ask yourself, "Where is my anger coming from?" and "Does something within me foster unnecessary and excessive anger?" As already noted, anger is a universal human emotion. There is nothing inherently wrong with feeling angry. Yet sometimes we experience extreme and pointless wrath. "It's not fair!" themes, which appeared in Kyle's unhelpful self-talk, commonly feed this disproportionate rage.

"IT'S NOT FAIR!": SENSE OF ENTITLEMENT

An overdeveloped sense of entitlement regularly stokes fires of anger and is a common form of "It's not fair!" thinking. Drs. Jean M. Twenge and W. Keith Campbell, authors of *The Narcissism Epidemic,* write:

> Entitlement is fun while it lasts. You live in a fantasy in which the world owes you more than you contribute. You can feel entitled to a flat-screen TV without earning the money to pay for it. You can park in the handicapped space because you are in a rush. You can graduate from college and expect to get a fulfilling job with a six-figure salary right away.[7]

But when the entitled are thwarted, they feel deprived and angry.

Mason's sense of entitlement reacted when his wife didn't want him to attend the annual golf weekend with his buddies because the finances were so tight this year. He felt outraged when Abby shared her opinion; he firmly believed he deserved the weekend regardless of their situation. Then he imposed the silent treatment and emotionally detached from her. He resolved to make her regret challenging the affordability of this weekend so essential to male bonding. She must suffer for this! Writing self-talk, however, forced him to face what was beneath his seeming righteous indignation.

Situation	Unhelpful Self-Talk	Feelings	Behavior
Abby won't support me taking my annual golf weekend with my buddies	I don't feel like talking *BECAUSE* I'm so disgusted with her *BECAUSE* she's always trying to control the purse strings *BECAUSE* she thinks it's her right *which is a problem because* (*WIAPB*) it's not fair *BECAUSE* she doesn't see how important this trip is to me *BECAUSE* if she did she would encourage me to go *BE-*	misunderstood	Shut down. Don't speak.

Situation	Unhelpful Self-Talk	Feelings	Behavior
this year due to finances. Considering whether to talk with her or shut down.	*CAUSE* it would make me happy *WIAPB* if I engage with her she'll think I'm fine with staying home *WIAPB* I really want to go *BECAUSE* it's my one time each year to golf with my friends *WIAPB* she doesn't care *BECAUSE* all she can think about is how much I'd be spending *WIAPB* she won't support me taking this trip. . . .		
	If I'm miserable, she's going to be miserable *BECAUSE* I won't talk to her *BECAUSE* she needs to know how mad I am *BECAUSE* she's trying to stop me from going *WIAPB* I won't let her control me *BECAUSE* I deserve to spend a bit on myself *which is important because* (*WIIB*) I have a right to this weekend *BECAUSE* I want to go *WIIB* I must get what I want.	vengeful entitled	

Writing unhelpful self-talk exposed the ugly flaws in Mason's thinking. He recognized he must stop indulging such self-centered interpretations of his situation. He used the train metaphor (see chapter 3) to remind himself not to allow feelings to rule his life, and the following self-talk helped him toughen up and deal with his financial reality.

Situation	Helpful Self-Talk	Feelings	Behavior
Abby won't support me taking my annual golf weekend with my buddies this year due to finances. Considering whether to talk with her or shut down.	I feel disgusted with her. I don't feel like talking. But it's time I remove feelings from the engine and put them in the caboose of my train where they belong. Shutting down solves nothing. I'm perfectly capable of speaking; I'll talk respectfully and stay engaged no matter how I feel. It's true: we don't have the money this year for the trip. We've always lived by the rule that we don't charge more than we can pay in full when the bills arrive at month's end. Abby has given up things she wanted too, like the health club membership. There'll be other golf weekends. If I start setting aside money now I won't miss out next year.	more contented more patient resolved	Speak to Abby—engage with her naturally. Share responsibility for finances. Start saving for next year's golf weekend.
	I won't coddle myself, using the silent treatment to punish. Life has disappointments—deal with it. The entitlement mentality just breeds anger. I have no *right* to a golf weekend; I *want* a golf weekend, which we can't afford this year. Reminding me of		

Situation	Helpful Self-Talk	Feelings	Behavior
	our decision to carry no credit balance isn't controlling me. It's wrong to relegate to Abby sole responsibility for enforcing a joint agreement that best serves our financial future.		

Facing up to a sense of entitlement requires tough self-talk. Unchecked, such self-centeredness not only creates unnecessary anger but also seriously harms relationships with others. Healthy people eventually disengage from those who believe the world revolves around them.

"It's not fair!": Jealousy

Jealousy, another manifestation of "It's not fair!" thinking, produces unnecessary anger as well. In chapter 4 we explored the benefits of the tenth commandment to mental health:

> You shall not covet your neighbor's house. You shall not covet your neighbor's wife, or his male or female servant, his ox or donkey, or anything that belongs to your neighbor.[8]

Jealousy feeds anger, alienating us from others as we stew over perceived inequities. We can all make choices: develop jealousy toward those who have more than we do or thank God for the many gifts he has given us. We can even decide to be happy for people with more. The consequences of these choices hugely impact our emotional health.

"It's not fair!": Hurt Feelings/Injured Pride

Sometimes an "It's not fair!" mentality sits at the root of hurt feelings and injured pride, once again creating disproportionate anger. All people have defects, and this is a basic premise of Christianity. Given that humans cannot escape their sinful nature this side of eternity, we need not react with shock or dismay when others point out our failings. Yet people often take offense and assume a defensive posture when confronted.

Recall Ella's response when her husband, Ron, spoke with her about her tendency to gossip (see chapter 4). First she denied his feedback; then she attacked him. Had she held on to this response, Ella would have missed out on an opportunity for personal growth. Helpful self-talk defused her anger.

Debra regularly felt offended too. She considered any gathering among her social circle that excluded her to be a personal affront. The pain she experienced whenever learning that two or more friends met without her was practically more than she could bear. Observe her characteristic thinking:

Situation	Unhelpful Self-Talk	Feelings	Behavior
We learned that the Smiths invited several of our other friends over for dinner. We weren't included.	I thought they were our friends *BECAUSE* we've enjoyed many great times with them *which is a problem because* (*WIAPB*) they didn't invite us to their dinner party *BECAUSE* they prefer their other friends *BECAUSE* they invited them and not us *WIAPB* if they valued our friendship they'd include us in all their entertaining.	insulted	Don't speak to the Smiths. Closely monitor their social life.
	It was rude of them not to invite us *BECAUSE* we always invite them when we entertain *WIAPB* they should do the same *BECAUSE* that's only fair *BECAUSE* good friends invite everyone in their circle every time they entertain.	entitled	
	I heard the party was wonderful *WIAPB* we missed out on the fun *WIAPB* we shouldn't have been excluded *BECAUSE* it's <u>not</u> <u>fair</u>!	deprived	

Through writing the unhelpful self-talk, Debra realized her anger was avoidable. "It's not fair!" thinking created her hurt feelings, a self-inflicted wound. She could find relief simply by choosing a more adaptive and equally believable interpretation of her situation.

Situation	Helpful Self-Talk	Feelings	Behavior
We learned that the Smiths invited	The Smiths are our friends and we've enjoyed many wonderful times with them. However, true friendship doesn't mean one never does anything without the other. I don't need to interpret their inviting a few	confident secure content	Remain friendly to the Smiths.

Situation	Helpful Self-Talk	Feelings	Behavior
several of our other friends over for dinner. We weren't included.	friends for dinner as a personal rejection. That has nothing to do with us. Besides, I must quit looking to others for acceptance and confidence. It's not good to give people this power over my sense of worth. The Smiths are free to entertain whomever they please. They have no obligation to always include us. If we've always included them when entertaining (unlikely), we aren't reaching out enough to others. It is healthy to nurture a wide circle of friends. We would be wise to befriend more people.	motivated	Reach out to develop other friend- ships too.
	It's ridiculous to think we shouldn't ever be excluded from a fun gathering. Everyone misses out some- times. This is life!		

"It's not fair!": Attempted Mind-Reading

Assuming we know someone else's thoughts likewise can fuel unnecessary and excessive anger. No one can read minds, not even long-married couples. Yet people speculate with confidence on the thoughts and behaviors of others, then feel offended by what they project on one another. Debra assumed the Smiths purposely excluded her, preferring other friends to her husband and herself, when the Smiths actually love them both.

Kyle, who opened this chapter with road rage, imagined the woman in the car ahead gloating over her success in cutting off his car. In truth, Kyle was the furthest thing from her mind as she stressed over driving through a huge and unfamiliar city to which she'd just relocated. Resisting the urge to assume we can read a mind may save us from needless hurt and anger.

Action 3: Describe the Person I Am Considering Confronting

After examining what triggered our frustration and whether our own issues created a disproportionate emotional reaction, we may decide to confront the individual with whom we're upset. But before doing this we are prudent to reflect on the makeup of the person we plan to address. Think about who he or she is, and consider the likelihood that confrontation would correct the problem. After completing these actions, we may conclude that, indeed, confrontation is our best option. On the other hand, we might decide such a choice is neither wise nor necessary. Being a truly authentic person does not require confrontation each time I have a legitimate gripe.

Confrontation is difficult for practically everyone to receive. Resolving issues with insecure people is especially tough, however. The highly insecure often respond to constructive criticism with shame and even withdrawal from others. Confrontations with manipulative individuals seldom succeed either, as they twist and distort sincere feedback beyond recognition. To help decide whether to raise your issue with the offender, think about how close you are to this person and the extent to which your paths cross. Unless the issue is of a nature that clearly requires confrontation, consider using self-talk to resolve the problem on your own in cases where the offender is someone you're not close to, someone you seldom interact with, and/or someone you believe would tolerate confrontation poorly.

I make no claims to have the answer on whether or not to confront. No hard and fast formula will always correctly identify the best choice. I only raise issues to contemplate before scheduling a discussion of the problem. If the offender is your spouse or your child who lives with you, though, and you cannot internally resolve resentment, you must be able to talk with him or her about your concern, despite his or her level of insecurity or difficulty accepting confrontation. Without straightforward ways to discuss problems when people are upset, destructive expressions of anger emerge—the silent treatment, sarcasm, verbal tirades, and so on.

The following "Gentle Confrontations," designed for married couples, provide a structure for non-threatening confrontation between adults in relationships of equal power. The method (also presented, without comment, in appendix D) can be adapted for other types of relationships as well. The ideas may sound familiar but require self-discipline to practice effectively. Note that these ten actions are a *subset* of the three actions above (Examine the Situation, Know Yourself, and Describe the Person).

Let's walk through this process with Madeleine, who addresses an issue with her husband, Carter.

Gentle Confrontations

Action 1: Determine whether you're in the mood (a) to vent your anger or (b) to resolve whatever bothers you and thus to improve the relationship. If you feel pent up with rage, then take time first to cool off by exercising or writing the Seven Steps so you can talk in a non-threatening manner.

People may desire the satisfaction of unloading anger on someone who remains completely receptive to their message, yet rarely is a recipient open to such dumping. A verbal tirade informs others of our anger but also motivates them to build a protective wall against our fury. During the tirade, the receiver focuses on how to counter the argument rather than on weighing its merits. To maximize the likelihood that he or she will seriously contemplate what we say, we must first work through our anger so we can speak without attacking. Running, speed walking, or other physical exercise before confronting consumes excess energy and helps us communicate in a non-threatening way.

For years Madeleine has picked up after Carter, who frequently leaves clothes scattered throughout the house. His habit has always irritated her, but today she decided she must address the matter. His closet and dresser drawers appeared practically empty as most of his shirts, slacks, and underwear lay on the floor or draped over the furniture.

Although Carter's behavior frustrates her, Madeleine is not seething with rage as she anticipates the confrontation. Hence, she believes she can control herself when talking and need not walk the treadmill first to work off steam.

> *Action 2: Ensure that both of you are in reasonably receptive moods and that neither faces a pressure situation within moments. (Timing, Timing, Timing!)*

Everyone knows that confrontations seldom succeed when one or both parties are tired or in an ugly mood. Nor do they succeed when one or the other just arrived home or needs to leave within minutes. Still, people commonly ignore these basic truths. Growing impatient or believing that hectic schedules will never offer a better opportunity, many dive in to confrontations that due to poor timing are doomed from the outset. Postponing confrontation until there's time to talk through the issue and each person is emotionally prepared requires self-discipline.

Madeleine would prefer to confront Carter at 5:30 p.m., the moment their paths next cross, but she knows they both need a little time to decompress after work. As this is no emergency, she chooses to wait for a better moment.

> *Action 3: Ask first if he/she is willing to talk about something concerning you, perhaps sharing a little about the issue you want to consider. Couples can agree in advance to discuss matters within twenty-four hours of when they're introduced, so if one is not in the mood or unable to deal with a problem when first approached, an alternative time is determined*

right then. The topic is then dropped until the chosen time.

Obtain permission to address the issue before starting the confrontation. This benefits both parties. At seven in the evening, when Madeleine sees Carter relaxing in his chair, reading a book, she presumes the time is right to confront—he's in a fine mood, doing nothing important; plenty of time remains before bedtime. Yet, unknown to her, he has looked forward all day to these thirty minutes for reading. Rather than simply launch forward, she tells him first of her desire to briefly discuss something together and asks if he's willing to talk now.

This benefits him because he can say no; he really wants this half hour to read. It also helps her, as he then needs to propose an alternate time in the next twenty-four hours to hear her out. Some people forever put off their spouse by claiming the time isn't right *whenever* a confrontation begins. This third directive requires listening to the concern within a day of its introduction.

In response to Madeleine's request, Carter asks to wait an hour and a half for their talk. She readily agrees and refrains from silently punishing him by emotionally detaching from him for the next ninety minutes. At 8:30 Carter approaches Madeleine, inviting her to share her concern.

Action 4: *Minimize defensiveness in him/her by appearing non-threatening. Watch your tone of voice. Avoid sounding accusing or patronizing. Also monitor your body language. Do not cross your arms. Face him/her in a relaxed manner.*

We discussed in chapter 7 the importance of tone and of body language. With voice, the most obvious confrontation concern is yelling. But making your point with unnaturally slow, deliberate speech sounds patronizing and may turn off the listener as well. Talk in a natural, matter-of-fact way. Many of us have transparent faces that broadcast any anger we feel inside. It's important to relax facial muscles and not appear ready to attack.

Madeleine knows she tends to raise her voice and talk quickly when she is the least bit agitated. As noted in Action 1, she is not overcome with anger right now. Yet she vows to monitor her nonverbal communications throughout this confrontation to help ensure that the discussion never escalates to a battle.

> **Action 5: *Share what he/she does right regarding the concern you want to address. If you feel he/she does nothing right in that realm, give credit for positive efforts on a related issue.***

Some people prefer to ignore action 5 because a "but" naturally follows. However, commenting on what you appreciate benefits both parties. For one thing, it compels the confronter to get perspective, identifying what the other does right. Pausing here, Madeleine remembers things about Carter for which she's thankful. Action 5 also conveys to him that she is reasonable and sees the good in him, so he senses less need to defend himself. If she just blurts out, "You leave your clothes around in *piles*," he'll reply, "But I vacuum, clean the bathrooms, and do much of the yard work!" Beginning by noting that he vacuums, cleans bathrooms, and takes care of the yard, she shows she recognizes his efforts and is fair-minded.

> **Action 6: *If you contribute to the problem you are presenting, or if you commit a similar infraction, acknowledge your part and vow to change.***

Madeleine often leaves her toothbrush, toothpaste, facial cleanser, and makeup all over the bathroom counter. She knows this irritates Carter. Hence, if she complains, "You leave your clothes on the floor," she can anticipate "You leave the bathroom counter a mess!" in response. Since she engages in behavior similar to what she's asking him to correct, she needs to admit this at the outset of their talk. Admitting her fault and committing to correct it before addressing the care and placement of his clothes diminishes his need to counterattack. It also expresses that she does not imagine herself sitting on a pedestal while he, a worm, squirms on the floor. For action 6, she says, "I know I leave the bathroom counter a mess, which bothers you. I will clean it off." And now she must follow through with her pledge.

>**Action 7:** *State precisely what bothers you. Do not*
>*generalize. Avoid "always," "never," and*
>*any other broad strokes when describing the*
>*problem. Stay away from labels (e.g., "you're*
>*insensitive" or "you're lazy"). Slightly understate*
>*the other's offense, for if you exaggerate at all,*
>*he/she may write off the entire confrontation,*
>*considering your claim unfair or irrational. Be*
>*straightforward, tactful, and specific.*

Perhaps most important to successful confrontation is avoiding "always," "never," and any other all-inclusive terms when depicting another's behavior. Even if Madeleine cannot remember Carter ever hanging up his clothes or tossing his dirty laundry in the hamper, declaring, "You *never* pick up your clothes!" will not likely succeed. Such absolute language sends people on memory searches for exceptions to the charges. Thorough reviews of past weeks, months, and even years often uncover at least one example of actions inconsistent with the criticism. Even one such recollection then nullifies the complaint. If she asserts, "You never pick up your clothes!" he likely will venture to recall the day four months ago when his laundry did not land on the furniture or floor, then dismiss her entire confrontation as unreasonable.

People often resist *understating* their point because they would consider this a *gift* to the person they're confronting. Understatement actually benefits the confronter, however, for it helps recipients hear criticism less defensively. Thus, if Madeleine cannot recollect one day without Carter's garments scattered throughout the house, she will say, "*Frequently* you leave your clothes on the floor or the furniture."

Madeleine believes Carter's transgression is "frequent," so she tells him, "*Sometimes* you leave your clothes on the floor or the furniture." She proceeds to offer examples of when his clothes have not been put away. (Here she runs into a bit of trouble, which she quickly resolves using a method I'll present in action 8.) She also explains how his behavior impacts her, noting, "I end up picking up after you, which frustrates me." Slightly understated language increases the likelihood that he will find her complaint valid.

> *Action 8: If at any time the person you're confronting appears defensive, do not say "You're getting defensive!" Instead, invite the recipient to point out anything in your style that does not work for him or her. Together you can then decide how to proceed before returning to the issue. (For example, the other person may say you are sounding accusatory or patronizing. You would then commit to stopping this tone and invite reminders if you speak in that manner again.) The goal is to keep the receiver's defenses down so he or she can hear your concern.*

Let's examine now the problem Madeleine encountered in action 7, while reminding Carter of times he left his clothes on the floor and the furniture. During this recitation she detected some defensiveness developing in him. Stopping right then to declare,

"You're getting defensive!" probably would not have removed the obstacle. People seldom respond to that observation with "You're right. I'll cut it out." Instead, they tend to counter with denials of defensiveness while building protective barriers higher and thicker.

If the other person appears defensive, drop the confrontation issue. Next, invite him or her to point out any problems with your manner of speaking. Upon noticing his defensiveness during action 7, Madeleine asked about her style of communicating. Carter then said she was offering too much detail about his offense, giving too many examples, and this was beginning to try his patience. After they agreed on a plan acceptable to them both—she would be more concise—she resumed confronting and spoke succinctly from then on.

Action 9: Identify the behaviors you would appreciate seeing replace the undesired behaviors.

After explaining the source of their displeasure, confronters sometimes neglect to specify how to correct the problem. In Madeleine's case, her desire is obvious: she wants Carter to hang up his clean clothes and place the dirty ones in a hamper. The desired actions are not always so apparent, though. For action 9, explicitly state what you seek from the other person.

Action 10: To confirm successful communication, the recipient restates both the problem (action 7) and the request for change (action 9). Any miscommunications can then be corrected. Finally, the recipient says whether he/she is willing to work on the issue raised.

Action 10 can seem patronizing, like an adult talking to a child, unless each party has agreed to this in advance. Yet both confrontation participants face challenging tasks: confronters must clearly express, and receivers must carefully listen. Verifying accurate reception of the message facilitates conflict resolution. Carter listened carefully to Madeleine's complaint and now, at action 10, he accurately restates her concern on the first try. He also agrees to put forth a concerted effort to pick up after himself in the future. She thanks him, and the "Gentle Confrontation" successfully ends.

Not everyone hears confrontations so accurately. Few people enjoy being confronted, and in the stress of the moment listeners easily misconstrue the speaker's intent. And, as previously noted, insecure individuals often exaggerate negative feedback in their mind.

Consider another married couple in the same situation. Like Madeleine, the wife is frustrated that her husband doesn't put his clothes in their proper place, but unlike Carter, this husband is insecure. Hence, he hears his wife declare "You don't love me!" when she simply tells him she doesn't like finding his clothes on the furniture and on the floor, asking him instead to hang them up or drop them in a hamper. Action 10 exposes his negative filter, providing her the chance to say "No" or "Not quite" and then restate her complaint and request.

Next this man tries again, declaring, "You don't think I contribute enough around the house," to which she once more responds, "No, I simply want you to hang up your clean clothes and put the dirty ones in the hamper." Again he states what he heard, at last asserting, "You don't appreciate me leaving my clothes all around and want me to hang them up or put them in the dirty clothes' bin." "Yes," she replies. Now she knows that he accurately received her message.

Then, he tells her whether he will agree. If he says no, they will need to brainstorm ways to solve the problem, identifying all possible solutions and their likely outcomes. Finally, the two of them will select the best resolution, compromising if necessary.

It isn't only insecure individuals who misinterpret confrontations. Manipulative people purposely do the same, taking issues to the extreme to derail discussion. Contemplate one more couple experiencing tension over clothes strewn throughout the house. This wife just told her husband that she does not like finding his clothes on the floor and furniture and politely asked him to put them in his dresser or hang them in his closet if they are clean.

He is manipulative, so he responds to her reasonable confrontation with, "I know, I'm a lousy husband!" This reply concerns her; she doesn't want him to feel badly about himself. Hence, she compassionately backtracks with, "Oh no, you are not a lousy husband" and proceeds to proclaim his greatness. In the process, she completely forgets her complaint. A wiser response to this manipulation would be, "No, I just want you to put your dirty clothes in the hamper and place the clean ones in your dresser or closet."

Unless this woman learns to remain focused like a laser beam on her point until her husband accurately repeats her requests, he will never address her complaints. Action 10 compels those confronted to state what they heard. This practice corrects not only simple miscommunications but insecure filters and manipulative ploys as well.

These Gentle Confrontations, whether precisely followed or loosely adapted to fit specific circumstances, provide a basic framework for addressing our frustrations with others.

Employing Relationships to Conquer Anger

Once again, *Take Charge of Your Emotions* demonstrates how three types of relationships—between thoughts, feelings, and behaviors; with Jesus Christ; and with people—can provide emotional relief. Utilizing these relationships may calm even anger, as this chapter has shown and the following discussion highlights.

The Relationship Between Thoughts, Feelings, and Behaviors

Our interpretations of life around us create our feelings, including anger. Thoughts and behaviors can feed rage. On the flip side, choosing helpful self-talk may provide relief and facilitate wise decisions in managing this challenging emotion. Regular physical exercise, a nutritious diet, and eight hours of sleep can also help relieve the stress often associated with anger.

Researchers have found that when we feel angry, we tend to speak faster and louder, which increases our heart rate, which intensifies our experience of anger, which causes us to speak louder and faster, and so on. By simply changing our behavior through slowing our rate of speech and softening our voice, we can interrupt this downward spiral.[9] When we choose helpful self-talk, we may produce the same effect.

A Relationship With Jesus Christ

Christ offers help when we struggle with anger. In chapter 3 we looked at the benefits of placing him at the front of our train. When angry feelings comprise our engine, we might spout off or shut down and punish others by emotionally detaching from them, often making matters worse. Conversely, when Christ guides our thoughts, which discipline our behaviors, and when feelings follow in the caboose, we may find relief from inner turmoil.

Jesus teaches us to love and forgive those who cause us trouble.[10] His instruction takes us to a place quite different from where trains powered by feelings carry their passengers.

Whether or not we feel like it, we can choose to obey him and behave as he taught. When we forgive others, regardless of the harm they may have inflicted on us, we release ourselves from the intense negative emotion that binds us to them. Choosing to forgive liberates us emotionally, improving our mental health.

Similarly, when our conscience convicts us that our words or actions have been out of line, we can quickly diffuse anger both in ourselves and in others by speaking three simple sentences:

"I was wrong. I am sorry. Please forgive me."

After uttering those words we must bite our tongue, avoiding urges to add, "But you contributed to the problem too!" and then proceeding to detail the other person's offense. Similarly, offering "I'm sorry *if you feel that way*" is worse than no apology at all. Those words only fuel anger in others, for they feel manipulated when under the guise of a gracious apology we refuse to own our error. If we can speak words that cause harm, we are perfectly capable of sincerely declaring, "I was wrong. I am sorry. Please forgive me." Silently counting "one, two, three . . ." can help propel those of us reluctant to admit mistakes toward vocalizing those words.

Certainly Satan recognizes the amazing power of apologies to heal interpersonal wounds. Perhaps that's why we often resist such a confession, listening instead to the tempter who argues that we must protect our pride, no matter the cost, rather than humble ourselves before God and others.

The following passages inform us about anger and how to cope with it.

> Refrain from anger and turn from wrath;
> do not fret—it only leads to evil.[11]

> Fools show their annoyance at once,
> but the prudent overlook an insult.[12]

202

A gentle answer turns away wrath,
>   but a harsh word stirs up anger.[13]

Fools give full vent to their rage,
>   but the wise bring calm in the end.[14]

Peter came to Jesus and asked, "Lord, how many times shall I forgive my brother or sister who sins against me? Up to seven times?" Jesus answered, "I tell you, not seven times, but seventy-seven times."[15]

[Jesus said,] "To you who are listening I say: Love your enemies, do good to those who hate you, bless those who curse you, pray for those who mistreat you. If someone slaps you on one cheek, turn to them the other also. If someone takes your coat, do not withhold your shirt from them. . . . Do not judge, and you will not be judged. Do not condemn, and you will not be condemned. Forgive, and you will be forgiven. Give, and it will be given to you. A good measure, pressed down, shaken together and running over, will be poured into your lap. For with the measure you use, it will be measured to you."[16]

All have sinned and fall short of the glory of God.[17]

"In your anger do not sin": Do not let the sun go down while you are still angry, and do not give the devil a foothold.[18]

We urge you, brothers and sisters, warn those who are idle and disruptive, encourage the disheartened, help the weak, be patient with everyone. Make sure that nobody pays back wrong for wrong, but always strive to do what is good for each other and for everyone else.[19]

My dear brothers and sisters, take note of this: Everyone should be quick to listen, slow to speak and slow to become angry, because human anger does not produce the righteousness that God desires.[20]

To the extent that we practice these difficult instructions, we experience more inner peace. Simply determining to resolve our anger before the day ends, as Paul teaches, provides a better night's sleep and less turmoil tomorrow.

No one is perfect. Christ offers us forgiveness for our failings. Through the Bible, God also imparts teachings that ultimately foster emotional health.

Human Relationships

Sometimes anger is best dealt with intrapersonally, through self-talk. Writing out the Seven Steps can reveal how we contribute to our problem with another person and challenge us to take charge of the thoughts and behaviors that fuel antagonism. For example, the Steps may uncover a tendency to emotionally disengage from others as a manipulative means of punishment. Self-talk can also reveal how we justify losing our cool and speaking hurtfully. You can contest and defeat rationalizations for the silent treatment and for cruel tirades with the Steps.

At other times, interpersonal approaches involving respectful confrontation are important to the healthy resolution of anger. Sometimes we need to directly address the problem with the other person in order to bring about healing. Ideally reconciliation accompanies these frank discussions, but that does not always happen on this imperfect earth. Jesus, our example for living, did not unite with all the Pharisees who sought to destroy him. While we must strive toward reconciliation wherever possible, whether or not we bond with our adversary, Christ instructs his followers to love and forgive. Such actions release us from the emotional prison of anger. No matter what injustice we have endured at the hands of others, we can still pray for all people, harbor no ill will toward anyone, and look to Christ to be our source of peace within any and every storm.

11

Finding Joy

Rejoice in the Lord always. I will say it again: Rejoice![1]

The United States of America was founded, in part, with a focus on happiness. The Declaration of Independence, drafted in 1776, begins with "We hold these truths to be self-evident, that all men are created equal, that they are endowed by their Creator with certain unalienable Rights, that among these are Life, Liberty and the pursuit of Happiness." Getting together with friends and family, eating favorite foods, traveling to interesting places, watching or playing sports, attending concerts, reading great books, walking outdoors, or remodeling the kitchen all may offer this reward. It can be healthy and wise for us to make choices likely to create this enjoyable feeling.

The Burden of Happiness

While the pursuit of this emotion makes sense for everyone at times, we also can become obsessed with seeking personal happiness. Some people conceive of a particular ideal, involving a goal, an achievement, or a specific situation, and feel anxious, depressed, or deprived when not living that dream. Married people may tell themselves they cannot be happy unless their spouse, children, or grandchildren change in a certain way. Single people sometimes consider marriage essential to happiness. Teenagers may believe they cannot be happy until they're entirely free of their parents' control. Retired people might decide they will never again feel happy, not without the challenging career that once yielded such satisfaction and praise, or the physical health that enabled them to sustain a desired level of activity. People struggling with finances may believe happiness is impossible unless they obtain more money.

Whatever their circumstances, some people habitually focus on how their situation could improve and on how happiness is eluding them. As they live each day, "if only" individuals fixate on what is missing—perhaps some past treasure or anticipated future joy. "If only" people breed discontentment within themselves and others.

Take Whitney, for example. Nothing satisfied her. "If only this were different" was her theme. She raced through life, always looking to what was next and awaiting change for the better.

During her first years of college, Whitney could not wait to graduate and work in the business world. She stressed over finding a boyfriend as well. Once she and Tyler began dating, however, she missed out on the fun of a new relationship because she longed for the assurance that they would spend their lives together.

After Tyler proposed, Whitney's assumption that married life was far superior to her days of wedding planning prevented any sense of satisfaction or contentment. She fared no better as an apartment-dwelling newlywed, for then she fretted over "wasting money on rent" and chafed in her impatience to purchase their first home.

Ever reaching toward the future, Whitney constantly missed out on life along the way. Now she worked half time as an administrative assistant; she and Tyler had two preschool children and were buying their first home, a modest three-bedroom bungalow. She viewed their current situation like this:

Situation	Unhelpful Self-Talk	Feelings	Behavior
Considering my life.	We're in transition now *BECAUSE* the kids are so young *which is a problem because (WIAPB)* I'm exhausted and frustrated *BECAUSE* all my energy goes toward work and them *WIAPB* we never do anything fun *BECAUSE* we're stuck at home *BECAUSE* the kids can't do much and we can't afford more day care or a baby-sitter *WIAPB* I can't wait until they're older *BECAUSE* then life will be better *BECAUSE* we won't be so tied down, *which is important because (WIIB)* people can't be happy when they have to sit home with preschoolers.	impatient	Plan for the future. Pace through the house. Snap at Tyler and the children.
	We need a bigger house *BECAUSE* we lack play space *BECAUSE* toys are everywhere *WIAPB* we won't be able to afford it for many years *WIAPB* I can't be happy till we're in our dream home *BECAUSE* then life will be easier and better *BECAUSE* big houses bring contentment and happiness.	unsettled	
	I wish Tyler earned more money *BECAUSE* we need more money *BECAUSE* then we'd be able to do what we want *BECAUSE* we could afford more house and a baby-sitter *WIIB* we'd be happier *WIAPB* I don't see him pushing hard enough for advancement *BECAUSE* he likes his job *WIAPB* life would be better if he earned more and cared more about our future *BECAUSE* money brings happiness.	dissatisfied	

Whitney was a chronic malcontent, having fixated on an ideal and believing that life constantly came up short of it. Dissatisfied with herself and others, her attitude eroded her emotional health and challenged her husband's as well. Fortunately, helpful self-talk began to rearrange her thinking.

Situation	Helpful Self-talk	Feelings	Behavior
Considering my life.	Life involves change, so in a sense we're always in transition. Yet I've got to slow down and appreciate the current moment. We're blessed and privileged to have beautiful children who won't be young for long. I don't want to miss out on this unique time. I can choose to enjoy these days and evenings at home with Tyler and the children.	grateful content peaceful	Engage more with the family, planning activities we can afford.
	My scenery doesn't determine my satisfaction. Happiness can thrive in a one-room apartment. Dream homes don't necessarily bring contentment _and_ are more work to clean and maintain. Our home won't be as cluttered if we train the kids to pick up from one activity before starting another.		Teach the kids to pick up after themselves before they start something new.
	Money's nice but doesn't guarantee contentment. More of it could bring more expenses and complications. Tyler isn't lazy—he works hard at the job he enjoys. Someday one or both of us may earn a promotion. Meanwhile, I'm choosing to focus on what's good about today and on what we have, not on what we lack.		

Here is the problem with devoting our lives to pursuing happiness. In addition to the self-centeredness that develops when this is our sole aim, making personal happiness our top priority sets us up for significant frustration and disappointment, because *happiness is a feeling.*

Feelings are fickle and fleeting. We saw in chapter 3 how unwise it is to place them in our train's engine; it's also perilous to select a feeling as our guide for living. C. S. Lewis recognized this human tendency to focus on our feelings. In his novel *The Screwtape Letters*, Uncle Screwtape, a devil, trains his nephew, Wormwood, to be an effective tempter and to discourage faith in God. As a part of his instruction, he advises,

> The simplest is to turn their gaze away from [God] toward themselves. . . . When they meant to ask [God] for charity, let them, instead start trying to manufacture charitable feelings. . . . When they meant to pray for courage, let them really be trying to feel brave. When they are praying for forgiveness, let them really be

trying to feel forgiven. Teach them to estimate the value of each prayer by their success in producing the desired feeling.[2]

Even when we go to great lengths to try creating the feeling, happiness may still escape us, for feelings are not directly within our control (see chapter 1). Declaring, "Feel happy!" no more inherently produces happiness than yelling, "Quit feeling anxious!" necessarily dispels fear. But our self-talk and our behavior *are* directly within our control. We can choose how we interpret life, we can choose our actions, and we can indirectly take charge of our feelings through how we choose to think and what we choose to do.

A Different Pursuit

Christ offers us inner peace and joy. Psychological tools can help focus our thoughts and behaviors on him, helping us experience him. Paul wrote, "Have the same mindset as Christ Jesus. . . . It is God who works in you to will and to act in order to fulfill his good purpose."[3] Almost two thousand years before contemporary cognitive/behavioral theorists, he identified those two factors directly inside our control: "will" and "actions"—that is, our thoughts and our behavior. He instructs us here to allow God's Spirit to work in us in order that we can *will* and *act* according to his best design for us.

Writing self-talk helps us understand and take charge of our thoughts and behavior. Including biblical truths in the helpful self-talk trains our brain to interpret life in a more constructive way. Reading the Bible and prayer assist us in knowing God and his purpose for our lives.

As we explored in chapter 3, we can find freedom from the pressure of seeking and maintaining personal happiness when our ultimate goal is to be an instrument of God. Unlike the unattainable or unsustainable circumstances we may deem essential to our happiness, anyone can serve Christ, even those unaware of how their life might be impacting others. Every morning we can pray, "Dear God, please use me today, and guide me in everything I think, say, and do." Then we embark on the adventure of discovering what he will put in our path. From focusing our thoughts and behaviors on serving him comes a deeper happiness—*joy*. Fulfillment and a satisfaction that reach to the core of our being often accompany these joint ventures with Christ.

Christians need not attain everything they want. An old commercial proclaimed, "You only go around once in life, so grab all the gusto you can get!" This thinking is quite the opposite of what Jesus teaches and promises. This time we have on earth is not all there is. We look forward to eternity in heaven, where there's no pain or deprivation. Hope penetrates even the bleakness of our darkest trials, for all problems here are short-term. In heaven, people will know complete joy that will last forever (see chapter 5).

Joyless Days

Aware of the joy God can bring to life, sometimes when followers of Christ do not experience joy they conclude that they aren't "good-enough Christians" or that God has abandoned them. But the reality of God's presence and of a relationship with him is not measured by feelings. We need not suffer guilt for feeling depressed, anxious, angry, or any other negative emotion.

At some time or another most people encounter trials that challenge their emotional and spiritual well-being. While unpleasant and uncomfortable at the time, such difficulties provide us with opportunities to develop emotional and spiritual muscle. We become more adept at using psychological tools through wrestling with significant tests. In addition, confidence in our ability to take charge of our emotions grows when we succeed in uncovering and turning around the problem-thinking that's contributing to our pain.

More important, facing seemingly insurmountable threats can strengthen our faith in Christ. It is difficult to recognize our utter dependence on God when worldly security appears rock solid. When comfortable resolutions are not within view, though, we can best practice trusting God entirely. Even our relationships with other people can benefit from times of trial. When we choose to share our burdens with family and friends, our bonds with them often deepen as well. The Seven Steps, a relationship with Christ, and relationships with people help us cope with emotional challenges and move beyond pain, preparing us for joy.

Employing Relationships to Find Joy

Sharing a vital two-way relationship with Christ and doing his will are a choice, not a feeling. Both are completely within your control, no matter how you feel and whatever your circumstances.

Paul wrote a very practical prescription for mental health:

> Brothers and sisters, whatever is true, whatever is noble, whatever is right, whatever is pure, whatever is lovely, whatever is admirable—if anything is excellent or praiseworthy—think about such things.[4]

And, I would add, *do* these things. Your thoughts and behaviors are directly inside your control. So take charge of your emotions by thinking and doing what is true.

Similarly, think and do what is noble. Think and do what is right and pure. Think and do what is lovely, admirable, excellent, and praiseworthy. When you treat others in a noble, right, pure, and excellent manner, you improve life around you, making your days meaningful and worthwhile. Instead of personal happiness, choose Christ as your top priority. Grow in your relationship with him, focus on serving him and others, and see what joy follows!

Appendix A

Seven Steps to Changing Feelings and Behavior

(*Note:* These steps are illustrated at length in chapter 2.)

Definition of Terms

Situation	Just the facts of what's happening (e.g., stuck in traffic, sitting in science class, sister is seriously ill, feel angry right now). A situation may be as specific as, "My phone was stolen" or as vague as "It's Sunday evening and I feel depressed."
Self-Talk	What we tell ourselves about the facts (or the situation). How we interpret situations—if our interpretation is believable—tremendously impacts how we *feel* and how we *behave*.

- Positive self-talk is often unbelievable and therefore has little effect on feelings and behaviors.
- Unhelpful self-talk is believable but leads to undesirable feelings and behaviors.
- Helpful self-talk is believable and produces emotional relief and healthier behavior.

We can choose what we tell ourselves about our situations.

Feelings	What we "feel"—our mood or emotions. We do not have direct control over our feelings, but *we can indirectly control feelings by taking charge of our self-talk and our behavior.*

Behavior	What we do. The actions we take.
	We can choose how we behave in each situation.

Take out two pieces of paper and draw four columns on each page. Write the defined terms as column headings, as follows:

PAGE 1

Situation	Unhelpful Self-Talk	Feelings	Behavior

PAGE 2

Situation	Helpful Self-Talk	Feelings	Behavior

Step 1: Describe the Situation

To complete this column, ask: "What is my situation? What am I facing?" Stick to the facts; keep it purely objective. Do not add your opinion or interpretation here. Use the same words on both pages (pages 1 and 2).

Step 2: Identify Your Feelings

Ask, "How do I feel in this situation?" or "How do I feel when I consider this situation?" Select two to six words that precisely describe how you feel from the Feelings List (see end of book); list them in the Feelings column on page 1. Choose words that have dissimilar meanings. In order to identify all the self-talk causing undesirable feelings or behavior, list every emotion you experience when contemplating the situation.

Step 3: Uncover the Unhelpful Self-Talk

One at a time, address each word in your Feelings column and ask, "What am I telling myself about my situation that's *creating* this feeling?" Write the self-talk linked to each feeling in the Unhelpful Self-Talk column. Avoid writing the words from your Feelings column in your unhelpful self-talk. Instead, use the words you selected in step 2 merely as *clues* to help you discover your unhelpful thinking.

- *BECAUSE*: Insert this at the end of any general statement. This device challenges any thought, draws out specifics, and demands that claims be supported with *detailed evidence*.

- *WHICH IS A PROBLEM BECAUSE (WIAPB)*: This phrase helps reveal *why* the previous statement is problematic.

- *WHICH IS IMPORTANT BECAUSE (WIIB)*: This tool challenges you to consider why your previous statement is *important* or *relevant*; it's often employed to uncover the reasoning that justifies engaging in undesirable behaviors.

Deciding which power tool to use is rather subjective; see appendix B for more detail. For now, try *BECAUSE* first to see if it exposes important thoughts. Utilize *WIAPB* if *BECAUSE* reveals nothing useful, trying *WIIB* last, when neither *BECAUSE* nor *WIAPB* produce valuable information. Asking "Which device will yield the most interesting information?" can help with selection. Continue digging in to your problem-thinking with *BECAUSE, WIAPB*, and/or *WIIB* until you repeat yourself or the thinking has become clearly irrational.

Step 4: Predict the Behavior

Reread your unhelpful self-talk. Then ask, "What would I *do* if I told myself this? What *action* would follow from this self-talk? What would my *behavior* be?" Write the answer under Behavior. To help distinguish feelings from behavior, avoid any words from the Feelings List in the Behavior column.

Step 5: Choose Helpful Self-Talk

Turn to your second page with its four-column headings. The first, Situation, is already completed. Now review your unhelpful self-talk from page 1, line by line, and address each concern uncovered in the unhelpful self-talk with a new, more helpful interpretation of your situation. Write believable (not just positive) helpful self-talk in the appropriate column. Fully unraveled unhelpful self-talk will often point you toward helpful interpretations. Use the following power tools to turn around unhelpful self-talk:

- *PROBLEM-SOLVING*: Identify a specific plan to alleviate a concern uncovered in unhelpful self-talk.
- *OFFERING EVIDENCE*: Provide facts to refute arguments set forth in unhelpful self-talk.
- *REFRAMING*: Interpret the situation in a more optimistic way while remaining equally believable (e.g., "the cup half empty" can be reframed as "the cup half full").

Step 6: Select the Feelings

Review your helpful self-talk. Then ask, "What feelings are created by it?" Refer to the words in the "Happy" column of the Feelings List. Record the precise emotions produced by your helpful self-talk in your Feelings column.

Step 7: Predict the Behavior

To complete the Behavior column, ask, "What will I *do* when I tell myself this helpful self-talk?" It can be useful, before completing step 7, to review those actions listed at step 4. Then contrast them with the behaviors produced by your helpful self-talk. Sometimes, but not always, the behavior following helpful self-talk is simply the opposite of what corresponds with unhelpful self-talk. And it may be that, rather than just one, several behaviors will follow your helpful self-talk. Write it, or them, in your Behavior column.

Appendix B

The Seven Steps

Tips and Troubleshooting

(*Note:* These steps are illustrated at length in chapter 2.)

A ppendix B provides tips (first main section) and trouble-shooting (second main section) for skillful use of the Seven Steps. Whether you are preparing to embark on a month of daily writing or want to employ the Steps once for help in coping with a difficult challenge, this appendix can serve well as a reference.

Additional Tips for Using the Seven Steps Effectively

With the Seven Steps, often the instructions for one will carry implications for others. Here I will present these along with the information about the original step under consideration.

The following guidelines will help you optimize the power of the Steps to produce desired emotional and behavioral change.

Step 1: Describe the Situation

- When you want to make a behavioral change, describe the situation precisely at the *point in time* at which you face the dilemma you will address in the self-talk. Include the *decision point* as well as the *circumstances* that may lure you down a path you do not want to travel. If you were trying to eat less sugar, the dilemma could be:

Situation	Unhelpful Self-Talk	Feelings	Behavior
It's two o'clock [point in time]; I'm hungry [circumstance]. Considering whether to eat some almonds/cashews or a candy bar [decision point].			

At step 2, then, you would select the precise feelings you experience at such a moment, such as "tempted" or "out of control."

Similarly, for the situation, if you were working to curtail a tendency to gossip, you might write:

Situation	Unhelpful Self-Talk	Feelings	Behavior
I'm with my friends when Maya's name comes up. I know some juicy gossip about her. Considering telling everyone.			

Again, for step 2, you would choose (from the Feelings List, at end of the book) the feelings you experience at that point in time, such as *torn,* or perhaps *justified.*

- When using the Seven Steps to motivate yourself to take a particular action, begin the situation with *Considering,* then describe the desired behavior. Examples include:

Situation	Unhelpful Self-Talk	Feelings	Behavior
Considering inviting my boss and her husband over for dinner.			

Situation	Unhelpful Self-Talk	Feelings	Behavior
Considering volunteering.			

Situation	Unhelpful Self-Talk	Feelings	Behavior
Considering confronting my son about his disrespectful behavior.			

Then, at step 2, identify the specific feelings you experience when weighing such a choice. In this last example, the mother considering confronting might feel reluctant, intimidated, and overwhelmed.

- Describe the situation from one point in time, using the same set of information throughout all Seven Steps. This is necessary in order to discover your options for dealing with whatever challenge you face. Additionally, sticking with one point in time through all the Steps ensures that emotional relief results from your changed thinking and/ or behavior, rather than from changed outside circumstances.

For example, if you use the Steps to diminish anxiety about flying to Atlanta, the situation must specify one point in time related to the flight, such as anticipating the trip three days before leaving, or waiting at the airport to board, or in the plane when experiencing turbulence. Then, at each of the next six steps, including uncovering the unhelpful and creating the helpful self-talk, you'll write from that selected point in time. If for writing the unhelpful self-talk you choose "In the plane, experiencing turbulence,"

221

Situation	Unhelpful Self-Talk	Feelings	Behavior
In the plane, experiencing turbulence.			

the same point in time must set the stage for the helpful self-talk. This compels the helpful self-talk to address the fears generated at that precise moment without, in this case, the benefit of knowing the outcome of a safe landing for the flight:

Situation	Helpful Self-Talk	Feelings	Behavior
In the plane, experiencing turbulence.			

• Write the situation in the present tense, no matter when it happened. If Paige is offended by the way her friend Lucy corrected her daughter's manners two months ago, she would record:

Situation	Unhelpful Self-Talk	Feelings	Behavior
Natalie and I are eating lunch with Lucy, who notices Natalie chewing with her mouth open and tells her to close it.			

This will then set up Paige to identify the precise feelings she experienced at that moment, such as *offended,* which will point her to the unhelpful self-talk of:

Situation	Unhelpful Self-Talk	Feelings	Behavior
Natalie and I are eating lunch with Lucy, who notices Natalie chewing with her mouth open and tells her to close it.	I can't believe Lucy thinks she can tell my daughter how to eat. . . .	offended	

Note that the unhelpful self-talk is also written in the present tense.

- Sometimes we want freedom from a vague, unpleasant mood that seems unrelated to any particular event or dilemma we normally would describe at step 1. In these instances, simply note in general terms the presence of the undesired emotion, like these examples:

Situation	Unhelpful Self-Talk	Feelings	Behavior
I feel down.			

Situation	Unhelpful Self-Talk	Feelings	Behavior
I feel angry.			

Situation	Unhelpful Self-Talk	Feelings	Behavior
I'm stressed.			

After writing the vague feeling as Situation, survey the Feelings List (at end of book) to label more specifically your emotional state. The feelings you select in step 2 will then serve as clues to uncover the particular unhelpful self-talk that creates your emotional pain.

Step 2: Identify Your Feelings

- Review the Feelings List (at end of book) to label precisely every uncomfortable emotion you experience in the situation (step 1). Then consider whether any of the feelings words you chose might result from the same self-talk and, if so, select only the one with which you resonate the most. For example, the feelings *neglected, unloved,* and *abandoned* could develop from the same self-talk. Similarly, *vulnerable, powerless,* and *helpless* might share the same self-talk. Choose just one of these. If you selected a group of similar Feelings words that vary merely in intensity, pick the strongest one for step 2 and leave the others. For instance, if you feel tense, fearful, and panicky, choose *panicky* for step 2.

The instructions for step 2 state to select two to six words from the Feelings list, but try to limit yourself to two or three unless you have a lot of time to write; otherwise you may become bogged down with lengthy self-talk. If you're addressing a core problem involving a host of distinctly different emotions, however, *list* each of them at step 2 and then *unravel* them all at step 3. Later, at step 5, turn around each problem thought revealed in your unhelpful self-talk. Unless you can afford the extra time when tackling complex issues involving lengthy self-talk, you may want to limit your writing each day to thirty minutes until you complete writing all Seven Steps.

- Sometimes we experience both desirable and undesirable emotions when contemplating a particular situation. At step 2, list only the feelings you want to change. For example, when considering scuba diving lessons, a young man might feel determined, intimidated, excited, and apprehensive. At step 2 he only lists *intimidated* and *apprehensive,* for these are the emotions he wants to conquer.

- Occasionally words from the "Happy" column of the Feelings List lure us toward problem behaviors; positive emotions can motivate negative behavior. When this happens, you must include these words at step 2, along with any words from the four negative-emotion columns so that in step 3 you can expose the unhelpful self-talk that justifies unhelpful behavior and hence bring about the desired emotional and behavioral changes.

For instance, a student who procrastinates might experience three feelings listed in the "Happy" column when contemplating whether or not to begin working on the essay that is due soon:

Situation	Unhelpful Self-Talk	Feelings	Behavior
Considering working on my English essay (due in four days).		**relaxed**	
		confident	
		in control	
		tempted	

Similarly, two Happy-column words may express how a teenager, at one time committed to waiting for sex until after marriage, feels when struggling with whether or not to have sex with her boyfriend:

Situation	Unhelpful Self-Talk	Feelings	Behavior
Considering having sex with Travis.		**loved**	
		valued	
		tempted	

Two of these may also represent the feelings of an employee who typically submits sloppy work to his boss:

Situation	Unhelpful Self-Talk	Feelings	Behavior
Considering stopping work on my report.		**content**	
		confident	
		unmotivated	
		bored	

Finally, such words may be required to fully characterize the emotions of an alcoholic who's considering having just one drink:

Situation	Unhelpful Self-Talk	Feelings	Behavior
Considering having one drink.		**in control**	
		optimistic	
		tempted	

Step 3: Uncover the Unhelpful Self-Talk

- Whenever possible, when writing unhelpful self-talk avoid using the word *it*, which allows you to stay in generalities and prevents you from specifically identifying problems or strategies for correcting them. For example, when a woman writes in step 3, "I can't handle it," she fails to define the issue or threat. To thoroughly unravel her issue and later turn around her concern, she must specifically state *what* she cannot handle, such as leading her work team, resolving conflict with her husband, or studying Spanish.

- The three power tools: *BECAUSE, WHICH IS A PROBLEM BECAUSE (WIAPB)*, and *WHICH IS IMPORTANT BECAUSE (WIIB)* help expose unhelpful self-talk. Here are more principles to consider when deciding which power tool to employ.

  - As stated in chapter 2, deciding which tool to use is rather subjective, but aim for the one that yields the most interesting information. As a general rule, try *BECAUSE* first and see if it offers useful information. If not, next try *WHICH IS A PROBLEM BECAUSE (WIAPB)*. If that does not uncover anything of interest, employ *WHICH IS IMPORTANT BECAUSE (WIIB)*, the tool that will be used least frequently but sometimes is essential to revealing unhelpful ways of thinking.

  - When choosing between these tools and determining what to write next, consider not only the previous clause but the entire paragraph and the feeling you're uncovering from step 2. Ask, "Which helps me best uncover and explain the feeling?"

For example, Jane (see chapter 9) is exposing the unhelpful self-talk that causes her to feel nervous about traveling to another state to attend college:

Situation	Unhelpful Self-Talk	Feelings	Behavior
Soon I leave for my freshman year in Oregon.	I've never lived away from home *WIAPB* I may really miss my friends and family *BECAUSE* I don't know anyone at college. . . .	nervous	

Now, at the end of each phrase, as she continues to expose the thinking that causes her to feel nervous, she asks
herself, "Which tool will best help me explain *nervous?*"
Following this last phrase with *BECAUSE* would uncover
nothing interesting—often when freshman first arrive they
know no other students. On the other hand, *WIAPB* would
help Jane discover *why* knowing no one makes her nervous:

Situation	Unhelpful Self-Talk	Feelings	Behavior
Soon I leave for my fresh-man year in Oregon.	I've never lived away from home *WIAPB* I may really miss my friends and family *BECAUSE* I don't know anyone at college **WIAPB I'll have no one to talk to if I'm having a tough time *WIAPB* it takes time to build close friendships *WIAPB* no one will understand me**. . . .	nervous	

Given all of this—that Jane will have no one to talk to
and that no one will understand her—she uncovers why
she feels nervous with another *WIAPB*. She continues to
choose power tools based on which one will provide her
with the most interesting information until the self-talk
becomes ridiculous or repetitive:

Situation	Unhelpful Self-Talk	Feelings	Behavior
Soon I leave for my fresh-man year in Oregon.	I've never lived away from home *WIAPB* I may really miss my friends and family *BECAUSE* I don't know anyone at college *WIAPB* I'll have no one to talk to if I'm having a tough time *WIAPB* it takes time to build close friendships *WIAPB* no one will understand me **WIAPB I'll be very lonely *BECAUSE* I'll be all alone *WIAPB* no one else will be in my situa-tion *BECAUSE* it's unusual for freshmen to go away from home for college.**	nervous	

Throughout the process of uncovering the self-talk that makes her feel nervous, Jane asks, "What do I tell myself that makes me nervous?" From start to end of the paragraph, this question guides her in what to write and which power tool to select.

- Be sure to continue digging deeper into your problem-thinking with the three power tools until you repeat yourself or the thinking has become clearly irrational. If you stop too soon when writing the unhelpful self-talk and do not unravel the thinking this far, you may fail to uncover important issues you'll need to address in a helpful way when you reach step 5. Exposing all the unhelpful self-talk that causes undesirable feelings and actions is necessary for emotional and behavioral change.

- Most people who embark on writing self-talk daily for a month initially have the sense that their thinking is problematic in a multitude of ways. Yet once fully unraveled, thinking that initially appears divergent often boils down to just a few core themes that occur repeatedly in unhelpful self-talk. This simplifies the task of identifying unhelpful self-talk and later, at step 5, correcting it.

Step 4: Predict the Behavior

- Unlike step 2, which involves referring to a Feelings List, there is no list of behaviors from which to choose here. Simply read through your unhelpful self-talk and ask, "What actions would naturally follow from such thinking?"

  For example, Mary constantly compares herself to others, particularly Ashley, a girl at school. Read her unhelpful self-talk and then note the behavior that naturally follows:

Situation	Unhelpful Self-Talk	Feelings	Behavior
Ashley is a great athlete,	Ashley's more gifted than I am WIAPB she's arrogant BECAUSE she thinks she's better than everyone else	jealous	Constantly monitor her to see what she's doing.

Situation	Unhelpful Self-Talk	Feelings	Behavior
really smart, and very popular.	*BECAUSE* she's so smart, cute, and athletic *WIAPB* it's not fair *BECAUSE* no one should have more than I do *BECAUSE* I need to be at the top of the pile *BECAUSE* my worth is based on being equal or superior to those around me.		Criticize her at every opportunity. Distance from her.

Lars provides another example of how self-talk informs behavior. He's irritated that his wife, Beka, asks him to stop by the grocery store when he runs his Saturday morning errands. Review his unhelpful self-talk and notice the behaviors that follow naturally from such an interpretation of her request:

Situation	Unhelpful Self-Talk	Feelings	Behavior
I'm leaving to run a quick errand and Beka asks if I'd "stop to buy two gallons of milk and some bread."	I wasn't planning to go there *WIAPB* I have a lot to get done this morning *BECAUSE* I need to repair the mower, prune the bushes, and change oil in both cars *WIAPB* I can't do this during the week *BECAUSE* each night we have something going on *WIAPB* I'm never in charge of my own schedule *BECAUSE* Beka bosses me around *BECAUSE* she thinks her agenda is more important *BECAUSE* she believes she's entitled to run my life!	resentful	Snap at her. Tell her I don't have time to stop for groceries.

Step 5: Choose Helpful Self-Talk

- *Problem-solving*, *offering evidence*, and *reframing* are the three power tools to assist you in writing helpful self-talk. (See chapter 2, under step 5, for more on how to implement these techniques.)

- If you have no idea how to turn around your unhelpful self-talk when writing helpful self-talk:

  - Consult the Seven Steps Topical Index (after the Notes) to see if any listed topics resemble your situation. If so, the helpful self-talk in that example may serve as a template for helping to turn around your problem-thinking.

- Consider biblical truths that may undo unhelpful self-talk.

- Talk with a wise and trusted family member or friend to gain a different, more helpful perspective on problem-thinking.

- Sometimes when writing helpful self-talk, you'll think, "Yes, but . . ." as you reverse your unhelpful thinking. Your mind will take you to more problem issues you haven't previously addressed in the unhelpful self-talk. When this happens, return to unhelpful self-talk and write another paragraph addressing your new concern. You want to expose at step 3 and then turn around at step 5 all the self-talk lurking in your mind that creates distress or discomfort.

Step 6: Select the Feelings

- When you review the "Happy" column of the Feelings List at step 6, the words may all appear too positive. If emotions like *patient, optimistic,* or *blessed* are beyond your current experience but you resonate with them to a certain degree, just add the word *more* or *somewhat* in front of the feeling word.

  Note how Evan (see chapter 9), who originally panicked when struggling to answer his first two test questions, modifies the Feelings words he selects for step 6. When considering how his helpful self-talk would impact his emotional state, the words *confident, relaxed,* and *in control* seem too positive—he's not quite there. However, inserting *more* before each word enables him to accurately describe his mood:

Situation	Helpful Self-Talk	Feelings	Behavior
I'm beginning my math test	It's not uncommon to need a little time to get comfortable and warm up to a test. I'll just keep reading through the	**more** confident	Read through the test and

Situation	Helpful Self-Talk	Feelings	Behavior
and I don't know how to solve the first two problems.	exam till I find a problem that looks easier. I studied and did fine on the homework. I'm not remembering right now how to solve the problem because I'm telling myself scary, awful things, making it hard to think. . . .	**more** relaxed **more** in control	start with the easiest problems. Concentrate on the test.

Often our progress toward feeling better occurs in baby steps. Words like *more* and *somewhat* placed in front of feelings from the "Happy" column tend to help us accurately record how our helpful self-talk impacts our emotional status.

- If you want to change your behavior, your helpful self-talk needs to create feelings such as *determined, resolved,* and *motivated.* If you do not resonate with those feelings at step 6, return to step 5 and strengthen your helpful self-talk.

Step 7: Predict the Behavior

- Reviewing the behaviors recorded for step 4 can help you identify what actions would likely follow from your helpful self-talk. Sometimes the behaviors listed at step 7 will merely be the opposite of those noted at step 4—as with Tom, from chapter 2. The behaviors that followed from his unhelpful self-talk about attending a work party alone were to avoid the event:

Situation	Unhelpful Self-Talk	Feelings	Behavior
Considering attending Rick's BBQ alone.	I can't handle going *BECAUSE* I'd feel stressed because I wouldn't know who to talk to *BECAUSE* I'm not comfortable spending time with my co-workers outside of the office *BECAUSE* I don't know them well *WIAPB* they seem to enjoy each other *WIAPB* I'll be alone the whole evening *BECAUSE* people will stick with their friends *WIAPB* I'll look pathetic *WIAPB* my colleagues will no longer respect me *WIAPB* I'll lose my job *BECAUSE* I'm not part of the "in crowd."	panicky	Don't go.

231

His helpful self-talk about attending, on the other hand, directed him to the opposite action:

Situation	Helpful Self-Talk	Feelings	Behavior
Considering attending Rick's BBQ alone.	While a few of my colleagues talk about getting together outside of work, I've observed nothing to indicate that the entire office is one tight social group. I've been with this organization five years so my peers are not strangers to me. Jack, Sid, and Maria are consistently friendly, and I can't imagine them excluding me at the party. I can seek them out. In the highly unlikely event that I'm rebuffed the entire evening, my career won't be in jeopardy. Each year at my review I'm told I'm the top graphic designer at the company. Impressing others with my social skills at the barbeque is irrelevant to my work product and is therefore irrelevant to my job security. . . .	empowered liberated determined	Go.

At other times, the behaviors that would follow will not simply be the opposite of those listed at step 4. Roger (see chapter 8), who learns that his mid-semester biology grade is an F, engages in passive and blaming behaviors in response to his unhelpful self-talk:

Situation	Unhelpful Self-Talk	Feelings	Behavior
I just learned my mid-semester grade in biology is an F.	Mr. Nelson is a terrible teacher BECAUSE he says I have an F in his class BECAUSE he can't teach biology BECAUSE others have gotten bad grades too, and they think he's a rotten teacher which is a problem BECAUSE (WIAPB) I'm stuck with a lousy teacher WIAPB there's no way I can learn the material BECAUSE Mr. Nelson can't teach. . . .	victimized	Passive. Blame Mr. Nelson. Take the F.

The behaviors that follow from his helpful self-talk, while certainly the opposite of "passive," involve solving the problem of the pending grade with very specific strategies:

Situation	Helpful Self-Talk	Feelings	Behavior
I just learned my mid-semester grade in biology is an F.	Most people aren't flunking Mr. Nelson's class, and only a few of us complain about him, so maybe the problem is mostly with me. I'll make an appointment with him to go over my last test, see what I missed, and ask for strategies to help prepare for the next one. If after meeting with him and studying hard I still don't grasp the material, I'll ask for help from students who are succeeding or look for a tutor. I refuse to accept that I can't learn biology. . . .	motivated empowered self-respecting	Make an appointment with Mr. Nelson to get extra help. If Mr. Nelson can't adequately explain the concepts to me, ask for help from students who do understand or hire a tutor. Pay attention in class and ask questions when I don't understand. Keep up with the homework and ask questions about anything I don't understand.

The more specific actions you can list at step 7 to correct a problem, the more effectively the Seven Steps exercise will bring about the emotional and behavioral change you desire.

Troubleshooting Problems Encountered When Using the Seven Steps

The next section addresses the problems you may experience when writing out the Steps. For each issue listed below, you will find solutions followed by full explanations of each strategy proposed.

1. The Seven Steps do not provide emotional relief or behavioral change.

2. You have not uncovered any significant unhelpful self-talk that explains your undesirable feelings.

3. Your unhelpful self-talk is bogged down with too much detail.

4. Your unhelpful self-talk goes in circles, repeating itself without uncovering any useful information.

5. *BECAUSE* prompts you to identify a number of different concerns; or, *WIAPB* or *WIIB* compel you to identify several reasons why the previous statement is problematic or relevant, respectively.

6. Your unhelpful self-talk is not yet repetitive or ridiculous, but it has wandered from the situation and become meaningless.

1. The Seven Steps do not provide emotional relief or behavioral change.

(A) YOUR UNHELPFUL SELF-TALK MAY MERELY DESCRIBE THE SITUATION.

Avoid writing unhelpful self-talk that simply retells the story of what happened in the situation you're addressing. Bart is suffering over neither being accepted into a physical therapy program nor making a wait list for the third straight year. As a result, his sense of worth is threatened. Note below how his unhelpful self-talk only describes what happened:

Situation	Unhelpful Self-Talk	Feelings	Behavior
I wasn't accepted into a PT program.	I wasn't accepted *which is a problem BECAUSE* (*WIAPB*) I applied to ten schools *WIAPB* this was the third year I applied to ten schools *WIAPB* I've never been accepted or made a wait list *WIAPB* I learned after my car accident in tenth grade about the difference physical therapists can make *BECAUSE* they really helped me *WHICH IS IMPORTANT* because (*WIIB*) since tenth grade I've wanted to be a physical therapist *WIAPB* I didn't get accepted into a program. . . .	inadequate	

Bart's goal in writing the Seven Steps is to restore his sense of worth after this latest round of graduate school rejections. To accomplish this, he needs to identify the unhelpful thinking that creates his undesirable feelings. Yet his unhelpful self-talk above retells his story while never explaining his feeling of inadequacy. To correct this problem and uncover his unhelpful self-talk, Bart must first return to step 1: Describe the Situation. Here he must concisely and objectively set forth what happened. In the situation he will set the stage to address his dilemma right at the point in time when his suffering occurs. See how he takes the essential facts from his poorly written unhelpful self-talk above and presents them succinctly below:

Situation	Unhelpful Self-Talk	Feelings	Behavior
After applying for three years to PT programs, I haven't been accepted or made wait-list status anywhere.		inadequate	

When considering this situation, he feels inadequate. The thinking creating this feeling must be exposed in his unhelpful self-talk.

Unhelpful self-talk is not a *description* of what has happened; rather, it involves *your interpretation* of this description— your interpretation of the situation described as objectively as possible. You must uncover the unhelpful interpretation in step 3 before it can be changed in step 5. Observe Bart's unhelpful self-talk below, in which he moves beyond simply describing his failed attempts. Here he reveals the thinking that creates his feeling of inadequacy in response to the letters of rejection.

Situation	Unhelpful Self-Talk	Feelings	Behavior
After applying for three years to PT programs, I haven't been accepted or made wait-list status anywhere.	My chances of ever getting in are minimal *BECAUSE* I haven't even made a wait list after three years of applying to many schools *which is a problem because* (*WIAPB*) I've tried my hardest *WIAPB* for the past ten years I've poured everything into reaching this goal *BECAUSE* this work is my passion *WIAPB* I'm not good enough *WIAPB* I'll never become a therapist *WIAPB* I'm a failure if I don't *BECAUSE* my worth is based on opening a clinic someday.	inadequate	

For Bart, explaining his feeling of inadequacy involves including some information about his situation. Yet his focus remains on uncovering the problem-thinking that creates his sense of inadequacy. Such a focus reveals the vital fact that he bases his worth on becoming a physical therapist. At step 5, he will need to change this interpretation in order to find emotional relief.

If you only describe your situation when writing unhelpful self-talk, you will not expose the thinking that needs to be transformed in order to achieve emotional and/or behavioral change.

(B) YOU MAY NOT HAVE PRECISELY LABELED
YOUR UNDESIRABLE FEELINGS IN STEP 2.

At step 2, take time to review the Feelings List. Reviewing the list helps people more exactly label the soup of uncomfortable emotion inside, which is essential to finding emotional relief. Sometimes people think they know what they're feeling and rush through this step without consulting the list, quickly jotting down general words like *anxious* and *stressed*. Then they proceed to step 3, where their unhelpful self-talk may remain as general as the Feelings words selected.

Such hurrying through step 2 can result in lingering discomfort at the completion of step 7. Unless you accurately name each feeling creating discomfort, you might not uncover in step 3 the specific self-talk creating the emotion. The Feelings words serve as clues to guide in uncovering your unhelpful self-talk, which, if unexposed and left alone, still dwells in your mind and causes torment.

The person who assumes she is merely feeling "anxious" and "stressed" may discover when reviewing the Feelings List that she resonates with *intimidated, powerless,* and *reluctant.* These more specific Feelings words will point her, in step 3, to the precise self-talk floating in her subconscious that causes her distress. Having uncovered the unhelpful self-talk, she can then turn around the problem-thinking at step 5.

(C) MAKE SURE YOU'RE CHALLENGING PROBLEM STATEMENTS
WITH BECAUSE.

Used incorrectly, *WIAPB* and *WIIB* prevent people from getting to the bottom of problem-thinking, causing them to just skim the surface. *WIAPB* and *WIIB* do not challenge the statements they follow. Instead, they assume that the previous statement is true.

For example, Candice may write in her unhelpful self-talk, "I won't be able to do my job." If she follows that with *WIAPB*, she presumes she truly cannot do her job, which might propel her toward a statement such as "I'll be fired." By contrast, following "I won't be able to do my job" with "because" challenges her to identify specific reasons why she could not fulfill her responsibilities. Writing "because my software skills are lacking" identifies a problem she needs to address in the helpful self-talk in order to experience emotional relief. If she is unable to pinpoint any specific reason she's incapable of doing her job, *BECAUSE* will help her recognize there are no grounds for this assertion and dissolve her worries.

2. You have not uncovered any significant unhelpful self-talk that explains undesirable feelings.

YOU MAY BE JUMPING TOO QUICKLY TO THE RIDICULOUS
WHEN WRITING YOUR UNHELPFUL SELF-TALK.

Unhelpful self-talk concludes when it becomes repetitious or when the reasoning becomes irrational or ridiculous. Mindful of this, people sometimes unnaturally and abruptly bring their unhelpful self-talk to the ridiculous. For example, Brett is unhappy with his job. When writing his unhelpful self-talk, he starts explaining feeling "trapped" with "I'd love to quit but I can't." If he follows that with "*WIAPB* most of my life will be unsatisfying," he will jump to the irrational too fast and fail to uncover unhelpful self-talk that's crucial to expose. Conversely, if he chooses *BECAUSE,* he continues to unravel the thinking that creates the sense that he is trapped:

Situation	Unhelpful Self-Talk	Feelings	Behavior
I would like to quit my job in accounts receivable at the furniture company. The economy is struggling, and unemployment is high.	I'd love to quit but I can't *BECAUSE* there are no other jobs *BECAUSE* unemployment is so high right now *WIAPB* I'll be stuck in this cubicle until I retire *BECAUSE* no other options are available *BECAUSE* I'm too old to retrain for something else *BECAUSE* I don't have enough years ahead to benefit from that kind of investment *BECAUSE* I'm familiar with other job options and the training they require *WIAPB* I will have spent my entire career at an unfulfilling job *WIAPB* most of my life will be unsatisfying *BECAUSE* I can do nothing to bring meaning to it.	trapped	

This very specific unhelpful self-talk identifies the barriers for finding other work that Brett must address. Potent helpful self-talk cannot be written without detailed unhelpful self-talk. Conclude your unhelpful self-talk when it becomes repetitious or by taking it to the ridiculous through a natural progression of confronting your unhelpful assumptions with *BECAUSE, WIAPB,* and/or *WIIB.* If your unhelpful self-talk does not uncover all you need to address in the helpful self-talk, you will not find emotional relief.

3. *Your unhelpful self-talk is bogged down with too much detail.*

You may be using BECAUSE excessively.

Sometimes *BECAUSE* takes you to a level of detail that adds no value or leads into a meaningless dead end. Observe what happens when Chloe (see chapter 6), a single woman considering attending the theater alone, relies only on *BECAUSE* to uncover the feeling *lonely:*

Situation	Unhelpful Self-Talk	Feelings	Behavior
Considering going to the theater alone.	I wouldn't have any fun going alone *BECAUSE* I wouldn't have anyone to talk to *BECAUSE* I probably wouldn't see anyone I know *BECAUSE* this is a large city *BECAUSE* many people have chosen to move here *BECAUSE* it's easier to find jobs here. . . .	lonely	

Using only *BECAUSE* prompts her to write irrelevant details about the city. The unhelpful self-talk explains nothing about her dreaded loneliness when attending the theater. On the other hand, note the problem-thinking she exposes when she employs both *BECAUSE* and *WIAPB*:

Situation	Unhelpful Self-Talk	Feelings	Behavior
Considering going to the theater alone.	I wouldn't have any fun going alone *BECAUSE* I'd have no one to talk to *WIAPB* people will be visiting with their companions before the play and during intermission *WIAPB* I'd feel awkward standing alone *BECAUSE* others would watch to see how I'd occupy myself during that time *BECAUSE* they'd be fascinated by my solo attendance *BECAUSE* it's very unusual to attend a play alone.	lonely	

This unhelpful self-talk uncovers a number of issues Chloe must address in her helpful self-talk in order to feel comfortable attending alone, including the intermission and concerns that others would stare at her because she is alone.

If your unhelpful self-talk becomes mired down with meaningless detail, *WIAPB* and/or *WIIB* may help you uncover the problem-thinking creating your undesirable feelings and behaviors.

4. *Your unhelpful self-talk goes in circles, repeating itself without uncovering any useful information.*

AGAIN, BECAUSE MAY BE THE CULPRIT.

Note how *BECAUSE* causes Parker (see chapter 7) to repeat himself when writing unhelpful self-talk about attending a Bible study:

Situation	Unhelpful Self-Talk	Feelings	Behavior
Considering attending a Bible study.	I'd feel strange attending *BECAUSE* I don't know much about the Bible *which is a problem BECAUSE* (*WIAPB*) others there would know more than I do *BECAUSE* I don't know much about the Bible.	hesitant	

By contrast, observe how following "others there would know more than I do" with *WIAPB* assists Parker in delving deeper and carrying his unhelpful thinking to the ridiculous:

Situation	Unhelpful Self-Talk	Feelings	Behavior
Considering attending a Bible study.	I'd feel strange attending *BECAUSE* I don't know much about the Bible *which is a problem BECAUSE* (*WIAPB*) others there would know more than I do *WIAPB* I wouldn't fit in *BECAUSE* only biblical scholars attend Bible studies.	hesitant	

When deciding between *BECAUSE*, *WIAPB*, and *WIIB*, continually ask, "Which tool will expose the most interesting/important unhelpful self-talk?"

5. *BECAUSE prompts you to identify a number of different concerns; or, WIAPB or WIIB compels you to identify several reasons why the previous statement is problematic or relevant, respectively.*

NUMBER THE ISSUES, THEN ADDRESS THEM ONE AT A TIME, CARRYING EACH CONCERN TO THE RIDICULOUS OR UNTIL IT BECOMES REPETITIVE.

Sometimes, when writing unhelpful self-talk, *BECAUSE* will lead you to uncover several issues to address. Or, similarly, *WIAPB* will induce you to expose multiple reasons why your previous statement is problematic. *WIIB* could compel you to list many factors that make your previous statement important as well. To find emotional or behavioral relief, you will need to explore each issue. If *BECAUSE, WIAPB,* or *WIIB* compel you to list a number of issues, number them and then address them one at a time, carrying each to the ridiculous.

To illustrate this, let's return to Jane (from chapter 9), who uses this technique when uncovering her fear of traveling far away for college. When writing unhelpful self-talk explaining the feeling *insecure,* she discovers she has two fears: she "might not make friends" and "might not be able to handle her classes." Each must be unraveled until they repeat or become ridiculous in order for her to fully understand and then turn around her fears.

Situation	Unhelpful Self-Talk	Feelings	Behavior
Soon I leave for my freshman year in Oregon.	I don't know how I'll handle being away from home *BECAUSE* I've never been on my own *WIAPB* I may not like it *BECAUSE* (1) I might not make friends, and (2) I might not be able to handle my classes: (1) I might not make friends *BECAUSE* I don't know how to introduce myself to others and show an interest in them; (2) I might not be able to handle my classes *BECAUSE* they might be too hard *BECAUSE* I may fail to learn the material *BECAUSE* there will be no one available to help me if I have trouble.	insecure	

In another example of listing concerns, Dane (see chapter 5) struggles with fears of terrorism. When uncovering the thinking that causes him to feel *vulnerable,* he writes, "I can't guarantee the safety of my family because:" and at this point identifies three factors that create his sense of vulnerability. Again, each must be fully explored for Dane to recognize his problem-thinking and then turn it around in step 5. Observe how he lists and then unravels each concern regarding his inability to guarantee his family's safety.

Situation	Unhelpful Self-Talk	Feelings	Behavior
Thinking about risks of terrorism.	. . . I can't guarantee their safety *BECAUSE*: (1) any of us could suffer an injury from which we'd never fully recover, (2) one of us could be killed, or (3) we all could be killed *WIAPB*:	vulnerable	

Situation	Unhelpful Self-Talk		Feelings	Behavior
	(1) A disabled person's quality of life is greatly diminished *BECAUSE* he/she likely is unable to participate in or enjoy some of life's best things *WIAPB* if this happened it'd be difficult to adjust *WIAPB* we couldn't handle or accommodate this *BECAUSE* no resources are available to help and God would abandon us.			
	(2) If one of us is killed we'll be separated from each other *WIAPB* the surviving family members wouldn't be able to cope *BECAUSE* they'd so miss the departed loved one *WIAPB* they'd be very sad for a long time *WIAPB* they'd never again experience joy *BECAUSE* their lives would be empty *BECAUSE* on this earth we have no purpose apart from each other.			
	(3) It would be terrible if all of us were killed *BECAUSE* it'd be the end of our lives on earth *WIAPB* we'd never see each other again *BE-CAUSE* this life is all there is.			

6. *Your unhelpful self-talk is not yet repetitive or ridiculous but has wandered from the situation and become meaningless.*

GET BACK ON TRACK BY REFERRING TO THE SITUATION AND YOUR DILEMMA. THEN ADD BECAUSE TO THE END OF THAT STATEMENT.

When writing unhelpful self-talk, occasionally people find they are wandering down a path that's taking them too far from the dilemma they need to address. The power tools of *BECAUSE,* *WIAPB,* and *WIIB* sometimes only lead us further into the weeds. When this happens, refer to the dilemma you're trying to resolve in the self-talk, then add *BECAUSE* after your statement.

Note how this technique assists a man who wants to stay in bed when thinking about a difficult meeting confronting him that day at work. The tools initially help him explain his lack of motivation to face the day, but at the point printed below in bold, he has adequately exposed his dread. Now it's time to get back to the primary issue of whether or not to get out of bed:

Situation	Unhelpful Self-Talk	Feelings	Behavior
Alarm went off ten minutes ago. Considering getting up while thinking about the team meeting today at work.	I can't face the day *BECAUSE* I'd have to address the conflicts between my team members *WIAPB* it'd be uncomfortable *BECAUSE* people are angry *BECAUSE* some aren't doing their jobs *BECAUSE* all they care about is collecting a paycheck **so I shouldn't get up *BECAUSE*** I can escape this challenge if I stay here *BECAUSE* if I hide out here long enough all my problems will go away.	unmotivated	

The phrase "so I shouldn't get up *BECAUSE*" brings this man back to the question of whether or not to rise and face the day. It helps him take his argument to the ridiculous. Following "all they care about is collecting a paycheck" with *BECAUSE* would have led to (for instance) "they don't have a good work ethic because their parents didn't teach them well. . . ." Similarly, following "all they care about is collecting a paycheck" with *WIAPB* might have elicited something like "they don't care about the team *WIAPB* we will never be an effective working unit. . . ." Finally, following "all they care about is collecting a paycheck" with *WIIB* would have drawn out "they're cheating the company." Unless he brings his self-talk back to the dilemma of whether or not to get out of bed, the Seven Steps will not help him achieve his goal.

Final Thoughts on Using the Seven Steps

Appendix B presents a number of guidelines to help you produce emotional and behavioral change through the Seven Steps. None of these rules is set in stone. Remember: when writing step 3, the ultimate determiner of which power tool to employ is the answer to the question "What helps me best uncover thinking that creates undesirable emotions and behaviors?" Then at step 5, ask, "What thoughts will produce the feelings and actions that I seek?"

Appendix C

I/O Exercise

(*Note:* This exercise is illustrated at length in chapter 9.)

Action 1:List each worry/stress. Be very specific. For example, it's too general to say, "My kids are absolutely impossible." Instead, record each problem you encounter with them, such as disrespectful talk, ignoring direction, failing in school, or making bad choices in friends. Leave many blank lines between each concern and space for a column to be added on the left side of the paper at step 3.

Action 2: Review each worry and list what is "Inside my Control" ("I") to solve the problem. Also identify what is "Outside My Control" ("O") regarding the issue. Again, be very specific.

Action 3: Decide which of the "I's" you will actually do. Then prioritize them, considering the entire group of "I's" you selected. Write beside each its number of priority. (For example, if you decided to address eight of your "I's," you would rank your priorities one through eight.)

Action 4: Take out your calendar and decide precisely when you will act on each priority. Set reasonable goals. Write the dates according to the order you choose. Be sure to leave yourself time for the unexpected.

Action 5: When you catch yourself worrying about any "I," remind yourself that you have a plan for dealing with it. You need only focus on your first priority; the others will be taken care of as detailed on your calendar. So you can let go of thinking about all but the first one listed.

Action 6: When concerns about an "O" cross your mind, remind yourself: no amount of worrying will in any way alter its outcome. If something is truly outside your control, then fretting, manipulating, planning, maneuvering, or losing sleep thinking about it will bring about no change. When you find yourself thinking about an "O," pray about it, leave it in God's hands, and focus your energy on the next "I."

Appendix D

Gentle Confrontations

(*Note:* This process is illustrated at length in chapter 10.)

Action 1: Determine whether you're in the mood (a) to vent your anger or (b) to resolve whatever bothers you and hence to improve the relationship. If you feel pent up with rage, take time to cool off first by exercising or writing the Seven Steps so you can talk in a non-threatening manner.

Action 2: Make sure that both of you are in reasonably receptive moods and that neither faces a pressure situation in moments. (Prioritize timing!)

Action 3: Ask first if he or she is willing to talk about something concerning you, perhaps sharing a little about what you want to consider. Couples can agree in advance to discuss matters within twenty-four hours of when they're introduced, so if one is not in the mood to deal with a problem when first approached, an alternative time is determined right then. The topic is then dropped until the chosen time.

Action 4: Minimize defensiveness in him or her by appearing non-threatening. Watch your tone of voice. Avoid sounding accusing or patronizing. Also monitor your body language. Do not cross your arms. Face him/her in a relaxed manner.

Action 5: Acknowledge what he or she does right regarding the concern you want to address. If in your opinion he/she does nothing right regarding that matter, give credit for positive efforts on a related issue.

Action 6: If you contribute to the problem you are presenting, or if you commit a similar infraction, admit your part and vow to change.

Action 7: State precisely what bothers you. Don't generalize. Avoid the words *always, never,* and any other broad strokes when describing the problem. Stay away from labels (e.g., "you're insensitive" or "you're lazy"). Slightly understate the offense, because if you exaggerate at all, he or she will write off the entire confrontation, considering your claim to be unfair or irrational. Be straightforward, tactful, and specific.

Action 8: If at any time he/she appears defensive, do not say, "You're getting defensive!" Instead, invite him/her to point out anything in your style that does not work for him/her. The two of you can then decide how to proceed before returning to the confrontation issue. (For example, he or she may say you are sounding accusatory or patronizing. You would then commit to stop using that tone and invite reminders if you speak in that manner again.) The goal is to keep his/her defenses down so he/she can hear your concern.

Action 9: Identify the behaviors you would appreciate seeing replace the undesired behaviors.

Action 10: To confirm successful communication, the recipient restates both the problem (step 7) and the request for change (step 9). Any miscommunications can then be corrected. Finally, the recipient says whether he or she is willing to work on the issue raised.

Notes

Introduction

1. John B. Arden, PhD, *Rewire Your Brain: Think Your Way to a Better Life* (Hoboken, NJ: Wiley, 2010), 18–19.

Chapter 1: Connecting Self-Talk, Feelings, and Behaviors

1. Reed, Mattie, Nora, and all other characters mentioned in these pages are entirely fictitious. Any resemblance of any such character in this book to any actual person, living or dead, is purely coincidental.

2. Aaron T. Beck and Marjorie E. Weishaar, "Cognitive Therapy" in *Current Psychotherapies,* Raymond J. Corsini and Danny Wedding, eds. (Itasca, IL: F. E. Peacock, 1995), 239.

3. Ibid., 240.

4. Ibid.

Chapter 2: Taking Charge of Self-Talk

1. When writing (and later reading) *WIAPB,* say, *WHICH IS A PROBLEM BECAUSE* rather than trying to pronounce the acronym. I use this phrase so frequently at step 3 that it becomes cumbersome to write without the shortcut.

2. As with *WIAPB,* each time you encounter *WIIB* say, "which is important because" rather than trying to pronounce the acronym.

At step 3, this phrase also can become cumbersome to write without the shortcut.

Chapter 3: Building a Solid Foundation

1. Psalm 103:2
2. The psychologist Albert Ellis, father of Rational Emotive Therapy, claimed that belief in God is an "irrational idea." The Duke University psychiatrist Harold Koenig uncovered evidence challenging Ellis's declaration, though, and his books present research from a number of universities that reveals the benefits of Christianity to mental health.
3. See Harold G. Koenig, MD, *Is Religion Good for Your Health? The Effects of Religion on Physical and Mental Health* (Binghamton, NY: Haworth, 1997), 50–51, 61, 64–65; and *Faith and Mental Health: Religious Resources for Healing* (West Conshohocken, PA: Templeton Foundation, 2005), 94, 110, 131, 146, 152.
4. Proverbs 3:5–6 NKJV
5. 2 Corinthians 10:5
6. John 12:26
7. e.g., see Psalm 139:1–16; John 3:16; 14:20–21; 15:9–17; Romans 5:8; 8:35, 38–39; 1 John 4:12–16.
8. e.g., see John 14:12–14; 17:20–22; 1 Thessalonians 5:10; 1 Peter 2:9–10.
9. e.g., see Jeremiah 29:11; John 15:5; Acts 20:24; Philippians 2:1–5, 12–13; 2 Thessalonians 1:11–12; 2 Timothy 4:7–8.
10. e.g., see Joshua 1:9; Psalm 91; 121; Isaiah 40:28–31; 41:10; 43:1–2; Matthew 11:28–30; 2 Corinthians 12:9–10; Philippians 4:6–7; 1 Peter 5:7.
11. Don Matzat, *Christ Esteem: Where the Search for Self-Esteem Ends* (Eugene, OR: Harvest House, 1990).
12. Luke 6:31
13. Romans 11:36 NEB 1970

Chapter 4: Respecting Hazard Warnings

1. Proverbs 3:7–8
2. See Matthew 7:3–5.

3. William J. Doherty, Ph.D., *Soul Searching: Why Psychotherapy Must Promote Moral Responsibility* (New York: Basic, 1996), 4.

4. C. S. Lewis, *The Screwtape Letters: A Devil's Diabolical Advice for the Capturing of the Human Heart* (New York: Bantam, 1982), xiii.

5. e.g., see Matthew 4:1–11.

6. Peter Kreeft, *Everything You Ever Wanted to Know about Heaven—But Never Dreamed of Asking* (San Francisco: Ignatius, 1990), 201.

7. Exodus 20:2–3

8. Exodus 20:8–10

9. Mark 2:27

10. Exodus 20:14

11. Exodus 20:17

12. Ephesians 6:11

13. Romans 7:18–19

14. Romans 8:1

Chapter 5: Solving the Unsolvable

1. Psalm 16:11

2. M. Scott Peck, MD, *The Road Less Traveled* (New York: Simon & Schuster, 1978), 15.

3. 1 Peter 5:7 NLT

4. Matthew 28:20

5. See Matthew 14:28–31.

6. 2 Corinthians 12:8–10

7. Kreeft, *Everything You Ever Wanted to Know About Heaven*, 151–152.

8. Randy Alcorn, *Heaven* (Wheaton, IL: Tyndale, 2004), 153.

9. Luke 24:39

10. See 1 Corinthians 15:20–23.

Chapter 6: Learning to Like Who You Are

1. 1 John 3:1

2. Psalm 139:13–14

3. Arden, *Rewire Your Brain*, 86.

4. Helen Keller, "Three Days to See" in *Atlantic Monthly* 151, no. 1 (1933), 42.
   5. Joshua 1:9
   6. Psalm 139:1–12
   7. Matthew 28:20

Chapter 7: Building Friendships With Others

1. John 13:34
   2. Alan Garner offers comprehensive instruction on the art of verbal exchange in his *Conversationally Speaking: Tested New Ways to Increase Your Personal and Social Effectiveness* (Los Angeles: Lowell, 1997).
   3. See John 12:3–8.
   4. Matthew 26:38
   5. 2 Corinthians 8:7

Chapter 8: Defeating Depression

1. Psalm 34:18
   2. Beck and Weishaar, "Cognitive Therapy," 239.
   3. Genesis 3:11–13
   4. Philip Yancey and Tim Stafford, eds., *NIV Student Bible* (Grand Rapids, MI: Zondervan, 2011).
   5. Psalm 42:5
   6. Proverbs 23:18
   7. Jeremiah 29:11
   8. John 14:1
   9. John 16:33
   10. Romans 8:35, 37–39
   11. Philippians 3:13–14
   12. 1 Thessalonians 5:16–18

Chapter 9: Overcoming Anxiety

1. 1 Peter 5:7
   2. *Panic attacks* and *obsessive compulsive-disorder* are two anxious challenges not addressed in this book. The conditions are similar, in

that fighting these types of anxiety makes matters worse. Panic attacks usually involve physical sensations, caused by adrenaline, that feel frightening. The more alarmed people become by these sensations, the more the adrenaline flows; this intensifies the sensations and causes them to last longer. If your doctor has ruled out a medical explanation for physical symptoms that frighten you and has diagnosed you with panic attacks, I recommend reading *Hope and Help for Your Nerves,* in which Dr. Claire Weekes explains how to turn off the adrenaline production that causes panic attacks. People who suffer from obsessive-compulsive disorder are tormented by disturbing thoughts. Desperate to rid their mind of the thoughts, they may engage in behaviors associated with the troublesome thought, hoping to end their mental anguish. (For example, people bothered by thoughts of germs wash their hands, expecting relief from their focus on germs. In the same way, people who worry about leaving doors unlocked will return to the door to make sure it's locked, hoping doing so will allow them to let go of worry about unlocked doors.) Similar to what happens when one battles adrenaline, the harder one fights disturbing obsessive thoughts, the more prominent they become in the mind. Dr. Jeffrey Schwartz's *Brain Lock* is the book I recommend to people diagnosed with OCD. Additionally, the Seven Step approach for turning around problem-thinking presented in *Take Charge of Your Emotions* may supplement the methods offered in *Brain Lock* and *Hope and Help for Your Nerves.*

3. Beck and Weishaar, "Cognitive Therapy," 240.

4. Ibid.

5. John 14:1

6. Hebrews 13:8

7. Luke 12:25–26

8. Psalm 27:1

9. Psalm 34:17–18

10. Psalm 46:10

11. Psalm 56:3

12. Psalm 62:1–2, 8

13. Psalm 91:1–4

14. Psalm 121:1–2

15. Isaiah 41:10
16. John 14:27
17. John 16:33
18. Romans 8:31
19. Philippians 4:6–7
20. 2 Timothy 1:7
21. 2 Corinthians 1:3–4

Chapter 10: Conquering Anger

1. Ephesians 4:26
2. Kyle did not write a separate paragraph for "vulnerable" because when he finished unraveling "vengeful," he realized he had exposed the thinking that created "vulnerable" too.
3. See John 2:13–16.
4. See Matthew 23:13–33; Mark 3:1–6.
5. W. Doyle Gentry, PhD, *Anger-Free: Ten Basic Steps to Managing Your Anger* (New York: HarperCollins, 1999), 13.
6. Ibid., 12.
7. Jean M. Twenge, PhD, and W. Keith Campbell, PhD, *The Narcissism Epidemic: Living in the Age of Entitlement* (New York: Free Press, 2009), 230.
8. Exodus 20:17
9. A. W. Siegman, R. A. Anderson, and T. Berger, "The angry voice: Its effects on the experience of anger and cardiovascular reactivity" in *Psychosomatic Medicine* 52 (1990), 631–643.
10. e.g., see Luke 6:27–29, 37–38.
11. Psalm 37:8
12. Proverbs 12:16
13. Proverbs 15:1
14. Proverbs 29:11
15. Matthew 18:21–22
16. Luke 6:27–29, 37–38
17. Romans 3:23
18. Ephesians 4:26–27
19. 1 Thessalonians 5:14–18
20. James 1:19–20

Chapter 11: Finding Joy

1. Philippians 4:4
2. Lewis, *The Screwtape Letters*, 11.
3. Philippians 2:5, 13
4. Philippians 4:8

Seven Steps Topical Index

List of Selected Tables and Charts

Feelings List

Happy	Sad	Angry	Afraid	Confused
Empowered	Devastated	Furious	Fearful	Bewildered
Motivated	Hopeless	Seething	Panicky	Trapped
Self–Respecting	Sorrowful	Enraged	Scared	Immobilized
Liberated	Depressed	Hostile	Shocked	Directionless
Patient	Apathetic	Vengeful	Overwhelmed	Stagnant
Blessed	Drained	Incensed	Intimidated	Flustered
In Control	Defeated	Abused	Desperate	Baffled
Determined	Exhausted	Manipulated	Frantic	Constricted
Confident	Helpless	Humiliated	Terrified	Troubled
Relieved	Crushed	Sabotaged	Vulnerable	Ambivalent
Pleased	Worthless	Betrayed	Horrified	Awkward
Loved	Ashamed	Repulsed	Petrified	Puzzled
Resolved	Rejected	Rebellious	Appalled	Disorganized
Valued	Humbled	Outraged	Full of Dread	Foggy
Gratified	Empty	Exploited	Tormented	Perplexed
Encouraged	Miserable	Mad	Tense	Hesitant
Optimistic	Distraught	Spiteful	Skeptical	Misunderstood
Invigorated	Unmotivated	Patronized	Apprehensive	Doubtful
Proud	Abandoned	Vindictive	Suspicious	Bothered
Cheerful	Demoralized	Used	Alarmed	Undecided

Feelings List

Happy	Sad	Angry	Afraid	Confused
Assured	Condemned	Insulted	Shaken	Uncomfortable
Excited	Guilty	Ridiculed	Swamped	Uncertain
Grateful	Unwanted	Resentful	Startled	Surprised
Appreciated	Unloved	Disgusted	Guarded	Unsettled
Elated	Degraded	Smothered	Stunned	Unsure
Respected	Pessimistic	Frustrated	Awed	Distracted
Admired	Discarded	Stifled	Reluctant	Embarrassed
Delighted	Disgraced	Offended	Anxious	Stupid
Alive	Disheartened	Victimized	Impatient	Torn
Fulfilled	Despised	Controlled	Shy	Tempted
Tranquil	Disappointed	Deprived	Nervous	
Content	Bored	Annoyed	Unsure	
Relaxed	Inadequate	Agitated	Timid	
Glad	Disenchanted	Irritated	Concerned	
Inspired	Unappreciated	Exasperated	Perplexed	
Satisfied	Discouraged	Harassed	Doubtful	
Peaceful	Hurt	Entitled	Out of Control	
Hopeful	Distressed	Deceived	Powerless	
Fortunate	Lost	Aggravated	Helpless	
Exuberant	Disillusioned	Bitter	Threatened	
Ecstatic	Lonely	Provoked	Pressured	
Terrific	Neglected	Dominated	Insecure	
Jubilant	Isolated	Coerced	Trapped	
Energized	Alienated	Cheated	Incompetent	
Enthusiastic	Regretful	Justified	Upset	
Secure	Resigned	Dismayed	Worried	
		Jealous		

Linda J. Solie (PhD, University of Minnesota) is a licensed psychologist who has been helping clients overcome emotional challenges and specializing in issues of depression and anxiety for nearly thirty years. She began her practice as a hospital staff psychologist working with children and adults and has been in private practice for more than two decades. A member of the American Psychological Association, Solie speaks nationwide at churches and retreats as well as other venues. She makes her home in Minneapolis, Minnesota.